What We
Can Endure

Louie Bottone

ISBN: 979-8-9939794-0-3

Published by Bottone Press LLC

Concord, North Carolina

For Ellie and Rosie

1
Nonno

"Did you find everything you were looking for today?" asked the bubbly cashier. Her genuine smile felt surreal, almost intrusive, as she glanced at me and my mom in the checkout line. *Didn't she know? Didn't anyone?*

Boxes of cereal, green peppers, and a loaf of bread slid in slow motion across the conveyor belt, waiting to be swallowed into thin plastic bags. The bags stretched to their breaking point before being stacked in our cart.

"Yes," my mom answered, fumbling through her purse for her credit card or some cutout coupons. The cashier lifted the cereal box and commented on the '3 for $5' deal she needed to take advantage of herself. Mom didn't respond.

"Thanks for being a valued club member, today you saved..." the cashier droned. Her impossibly wide grin lingered as I glared up at her. *Does she not know what just happened? Why are you smiling?*

The shopping cart rattled across the parking lot and toward our car. For an October afternoon in New Jersey, it should not have been this picturesque. One lone cloud dotted the otherwise unbroken blue sky as I climbed into our brown-gold Pontiac. A pop song burst through the speakers, only to be silenced seconds later by Mom's hand on the dial. She rolled open the windows and reversed out of our parking space.

Across from the shopping mall, I saw kids from school playing pickup basketball at the park. With the music gone, I could hear the bouncing of the ball hard against the pavement and the pleading of 'I'm open, I'm open!' cutting through the air. The world went on, careless and ordinary. But this was not an ordinary day.

The car ride was quiet as we turned into my grandparent's driveway. *Do I still say 'grandparents?'* Past the fence and into the backyard, I could make out the overgrown garden. In the corner, my grandpa's shovel still stood, blade buried in the dirt. Who would tend to the garden now that he's gone?

For months, the garden had gone untended. Nonno had been battling lung cancer for over a year before he passed. A lifelong smoker right off the boat from Italy, I can still picture him pacing up and down the oversized backyard, inspecting the zucchini, eggplants, and figs. He moved slowly, with intention, as though every harvest were a small triumph.

Despite months of neglect, the garden clung to life, though I knew it wouldn't last forever. My grandmother, nearing her eighties, struggled to walk on her own. She mostly settled for the grocery store vegetables these days.

But every now and then, she would shuffle into the backyard, stopping to pick out the brightest tomato or pepper. Just last week, she cut one open and told me how the grocery store varieties could never compare to Nonno's harvest. She stared out the kitchen window as she said it, holding back tears. It was the first time I realized Nonno really was going to die.

I was 17 years old when he passed; it was my first encounter with death. When my parents delivered the news, it felt like the world stopped moving. They said something about 'going to heaven,' but the words did nothing to console me. I was completely fixated on the idea of death itself. He was here yesterday. He is not here today.

What unsettled me most was watching his decline unfold. Nonno remained sharp until the very end, which is what we all wish for in our final days. But physically, his downfall was disastrous. The cancer had stolen his ability to breathe months before his last breath. The muscles he had built from decades of physical labor seemed to melt away in weeks. The proud, measured stride I had seen countless times in the garden was reduced to a frail limp by the summer of 2007.

Nonno completely lost control of his body in the end. The last time I visited him before his death, he seemed already gone. He sat slumped in the recliner where, as a child, I once perched on the lap of a giant. But now, I now saw a defeated man. I listened to my grandma tell my parents about how she was awake the entire night cleaning up the soiled bedsheets and floor. Death had arrived like an unrelenting wrecking ball, hammering at his door until it was splintered into unrecognizable pieces.

No one deserves an end like this, I remember thinking as I watched my grandpa's face sink down in embarrassment, unable to make eye contact with the rest of the room.

But what did 'deserve' even mean? Did it imply someone or something was doing this to him? Was there a series of decisions or life choices that justified this kind of end?

Nonno was a great man. He worked hard, provided for his family, and sacrificed so much to build a life in the US. Why, then, was *this* the sum of all that? Like death arriving at his doorstep, these questions battered at my mind with a force that made it impossible to think of anything else. *He was here yesterday. He is not here today. Why? And why like this?*

I felt like the only person in the world who didn't understand what was happening. Worse still, death and dying were taboo topics that were not discussed in my family. In fact, in those moments, I realized death and dying were taboo topics *everywhere*. How was everyone else so accepting of this? How did they go about their day when they knew the clock was running out? How did the grocery store cashier bag peppers without thinking about her impending doom? And why are we buying bread at a time like this?!

Yet here I stood, watching Mom slice bread for bruschetta to serve family and friends that came to pay their respects. Like life itself, the mourners came and went. I overheard the usual refrains: 'he's in a better place' or 'he's with his parents now.' Instead of acknowledging the brevity, the suffering, or even the sheer injustice of it all, the room filled with platitudes.

Everyone said what they were supposed to say in moments like this, and who could blame them? After all, we were a grieving family. These weren't questions to be answered or debates to be had. These were accepted facts of life. You are born, you live, you die, then you float up to Heaven if the big man in the clouds was pleased with your life's choices. Or so I was told.

At 17, I never had the chance to think through, let alone discuss, the questions now flooding my mind. For most, this might be where a religious community or set of shared beliefs steps in to provide comfort. But that wasn't an option for me. Whereas my Italian grandparents faithfully watched the Pope's mass from their television every Sunday and made the sign of the cross before every meal, my immediate family was less devout.

My parents were something like cafeteria Christians: take a little of this, leave a little of that, and fix a plate with whatever ideas were most appetizing. Sure, we attended mass on holidays, but even that was a rarity over these past few years. They might have claimed religion in name, but the only prayer said in our home was 'God bless you' after a sneeze. Looking back, I can see that they were doing what so many people do: keeping what brought comfort, discarding what felt hollow, and trying their best to piece together something that made life a little more livable.

Once, a distant cousin visited from Italy. She was a nun. I remember my Dad dusting off an old crucifix to put on the fireplace mantle. Some philosophers debate Pascal's wager, but I watched my Dad enact it in real time. If the reward was the pearly gates, then a little mantle space was a small price to pay. The crucifix was promptly shoved back in the attic once she left.

It is probably no surprise, then, that by high school, I was decidedly nonreligious. I don't know what I believed in, but it certainly was not what I learned in my CCD classes. Even so, I went through my confirmation. At 14 years old and already claiming agnosticism, I chose Saint Maximus as my confirmation name. Mind you, I had no idea who Saint Maximus was. It was the early 2000s, the movie *Gladiator* had just come out, and Russell Crowe made that name look so damn cool. If I was going to hell for being a nonbeliever, I might as well do it in style. Louie Maximus Bottone. That, I thought, was badass.

Yet as I heard the confident affirmations of "he's with God now," I wondered if somewhere along the way I had lost the plot. I had no framework, no ultimate source of truth, and no faith to anchor me in answers to these questions. Was it actually taboo to discuss death, dying, and the unfairness of life? Or did everyone else already have the answers, hidden somewhere in the Hail Mary prayer?

Even if they did, I realized the leap to accepting those answers was something I was not physically or mentally capable of. To believe that Nonno's passing was part of a divine plan meant also believing that his final, brutal days were also part of that plan. Whoever or whatever created the universe had signed off on months of suffocating pain that could've easily been avoided. This never sat well with me.

Surely, an all knowing, all powerful, just, and good creator could have imagined a more merciful way for Nonno to leave this world, right? If God didn't know how this was unfolding, then he wasn't all knowing. If he couldn't intervene, then he wasn't all powerful. If he could intervene but chose not to...well, that hardly seemed like the definition of a good and just God. No matter how I tried to force rationality into the equation, all roads ended in contradiction.

Eventually, I concluded it was all randomness. That's all it was. Biological functions gone rogue, with no higher purpose or hidden meaning. Unfortunate? Absolutely. But was there a divine purpose to soiled bedsheets, or a silver lining to the excruciating pain my grandfather endured? No. Of course not. Still, that wasn't the sort of conclusion you shared in the days after a loved one's death.

Nonno's funeral was the first I had ever attended. The room was ice cold and smelled of cleaning products laced with chemical embalming fluids. Polaroid pictures hung along the wall, and the space was packed with family and friends swapping stories about this great man. Now and then, a laugh would break through the otherwise heavy air.

Funerals are fascinating in that way. Some mourn the loss, others confront their own mortality, and still others act as if the coffin isn't even there. Like the lemon-mint cleaning product masking the chemical cocktail, platitudes and small talked served as distractions from the coffin in the room. Far from a chance to strip the taboo away from death, the event felt like an invitation to kick the can further down the road: *No time to discuss the inevitability of death today, I'm grieving.*

In the weeks that followed the ceremony, my hunger grew exponentially for something, *anything,* that could make sense of the questions keeping me awake at night. I was grieving, yes, but more than that, I was searching. Not just for comfort, but for meaning.

On one hand, I was reeling from a loss I couldn't process rationally. On the other, I felt an urgent pull toward purpose. If my own end looked anything like Nonno's, what did the choices I made now really amount to? How could anything matter if suffering was the final punctuation mark? I needed a framework: something to help me hold the fleeting nature of today while laying the groundwork for a better tomorrow. I didn't know it then, but the way I wrestled with life's questions as a teenager would become more than just a passing phase. It would shape the very lens through which I'd one day confront the unimaginable.

If death could strip away so much meaning, then I wanted a discipline that would force me to build it back piece by piece.

That search sharpened as I approached college. I wanted clarity, rationality, and logic, and craved a place where life's unanswerable questions could be asked aloud. On a whim, I enrolled in an introductory philosophy course. On the first day, the professor posed a deceptively simple question: "What's the difference between knowledge and wisdom?" What followed was a 150-minute, uninterrupted discussion.

The back-and-forth with my peers left me on the edge of my seat. Each time the conversation stalled, the professor would toss out another question, pushing us deeper and turning up the heat. *This* was what I had been searching for. I wasn't just forming foundational ideas about meaning; I was forced to test them, reshape them, and sometimes abandon them altogether. Logic and rationality were the baseline in that classroom. What set the truly skilled apart was their willingness to let go of cherished beliefs in the pursuit of sturdier ground. To make sense of today and survive tomorrow, I needed a way to interrogate the past. That meant practicing independent thinking: examining evidence, questioning assumptions, and drawing conclusions that could actually hold up under scrutiny.

By the next afternoon, I was hooked. My schedule was filled with *Ethics* on Tuesdays, *World Religions* on Wednesdays, and *The Philosophy of Death* on Thursdays. After hours, I huddled in the library with friends, carrying on debates that class time never seemed long enough for.

My undergraduate degree in Finance felt like an afterthought. A desk job in business was a necessary way to earn a paycheck, but my real focus was elsewhere: philosophy. I breezed through classes like *Financial Modeling,* spending more time wondering what Plato really meant in his *Allegory of the Cave.* Finance offered the certainty of equations and outcomes, but it was also cold and mechanical. Philosophy, by contrast, was a bottomless well for this new unending thirst. It offered a different kind of certainty: not the rigid validation of old beliefs, but the confidence that came from learning how to think, how to process, and how to act. I was captivated. What began as curiosity was quickly becoming the scattered building blocks of a life framework. Now I needed to assemble them.

From Socrates, I learned the value of questioning everything and choosing humility over false confidence. Kant taught me about moral worth and doing what's right, not what's easy. Perhaps my favorite, Spinoza, reminded me that true liberty is living by reason, not emotion; peace comes from accepting the world as it is. Reading these minefields of wisdom was both exhilarating and overwhelming. Each philosopher handed me a flash card version of truth, but integrating their ideas into daily life was another matter. I could ace an exam or draft a persuasive essay about these ideas. But how could I live by these principles?

Then, one fall day during my senior year, I stumbled upon Marcus Aurelius' *Meditations*. It felt like the greatest hits album of everything I had ever loved about philosophy. The Stoic guidance on reason, virtue, and discipline provided not just ideas, but a framework. Aurelius wasn't posturing or hiding behind abstraction; he was simply a man writing to himself, trying to live well. His words weren't lofty theory; they were practical wisdom. I read through habits and reminders for the everyday struggles of being human and felt as if he were writing *to* me. For the first time, I had language for the half-formed intuitions that had been floating in my mind. The books I had read, the late-night debates with friends, and the quiet moments of reflection all seemed to click into place around Stoicism. Even if I couldn't have articulated it in those terms at the time, I knew I had found something I could live by.

As graduation approached, I didn't feel like I had all the answers. But I did feel certain that I was ready for whatever life would throw my way.

I was wrong.

2
Family Fortune

We spend our earliest years trying to make sense of life. I spent many of mine trying to make sense of endings. What we fail to realize is that life is mostly made up of beginnings. The death of my grandfather cracked something open in me: a need to understand, to ground myself, to build meaning out of the chaos. By college, I thought I found that in books and ideas. Maybe I had. But what I didn't expect was to find that in a person. Somewhere after the lectures and late nights, the applications and job interviews, I met someone who didn't just tolerate my questions, but asked her own. In that beautiful aftermath, I met the person who would change everything: my wife, Emily.

In Emily, I found someone who shared my values and priorities in life. We both came from tight-knit families, spent most of our time trying to make each other laugh, and were equally committed to squeezing every last drop from life's experiences. Within weeks, we had already made a list of a hundred things we wanted to do together - from desserts-only dinners to movie nights to taking extravagant vacations we couldn't afford yet. But it wasn't the lofty plans that made me fall for Emily. It was the small moments in between.

The glance and smirk from across the dinner table when we both had the same joke in mind. The way the sun lit her face during our first trip to the beach. The way she played with my baby cousin at the family barbecue. Emily wasn't like anyone else. A month in, we said 'I love you.' By then, I already knew we would be married.

That day came almost two years later, in the summer of 2017. At the wedding altar, my cousin and best man, Michael, swears he heard me audibly gasp when Emily walked down the aisle. I don't remember making a sound, but I do remember the feeling of disbelief. I was marrying the woman of my dreams. Emily represented meaning, purpose, and our future, giving me confidence in the life we would build together. We spent our honeymoon in Aruba, lounging on white sand beaches, diving off cliffs, and imagining the years to come. Aruba calls itself 'the happiest island.' I couldn't have agreed more.

If marriage was the beginning of building a life, becoming a parent was the chance to bring a new life into a world I barely understood. The questions that once haunted me about death, meaning, and what it all amounted to didn't disappear. They simply changed shape. The framework and purpose I craved were no longer just about me. I would be responsible for shaping what it might mean for someone else. Daunting as it was, I was thrilled by the idea of fatherhood.

The first time Emily and I saw the grainy black and white images on the ultrasound screen, we fell in love. Fears and questions gave way to unconditional devotion for this tiny life. Every philosopher I admired cautioned me against the pull of unchecked emotions, but I was certain they would change their mind if they heard the steady thump of that heartbeat echoing through the speakers.

In the weeks that followed, I wasn't thinking about frameworks for approaching life or grand questions of meaning. I was consumed by preparing to become a father. I embodied every cliche about an anxious first-time Dad. My mornings were spent with parenting books and reviews of car seats; my nights with premature baby-proofing tasks. I built the crib when Emily was just a few months pregnant, nearly a year before it would be needed. Yet, seeing it there in the corner of the room transformed the space. What had been a guest room was now the place where a new life would begin. It had to be perfect.

When people asked whether we were hoping for a boy or girl, we gave them an honest answer: all we wanted was a healthy baby. And it was true. But I couldn't contain my excitement when we found out that, come December of 2019, we'd be welcoming a daughter. In an instant, I pictured daddy-daughter school breakfasts, bedtime stories, and the song we might dance to at her wedding. Days later, those blurry photos on the ultrasound had a name: Eleanor Juliette Bottone. 'Ellie,' for short.

At night, Emily and I would lie awake talking about the parents we hoped to be. Our approaches fit together like puzzle pieces. Emily focused on the tactical: sleep training, baby-led weening, and tummy time. I, predictably, went strategic. Before Ellie was the size of a grapefruit, I was already researching how to communicate with toddlers in ways to support their development. As a team, Emily and I were gaining confidence that we'd be able to survive, and maybe even thrive, in our first year as parents.

Emily kept her attention on the immediate: how we might get through the sleepless nights, feeding schedules, and formula choices. My mind, still in awe at the idea of fatherhood, raced years ahead. I thought constantly about how we could raise Ellie to be independent, curious, and kind. I didn't recognize it at the time, but I was searching again for a framework, just like I had done years ago as a young adult. Only this time, it wasn't for me. It had to be perfect for Ellie.

I wouldn't let her grow into the world unequipped to handle its questions and contradictions. Instead, I set out to give her an arsenal of logic, wonder, resilience, and skepticism. My job as a father, I knew, was to protect, prepare, and love unconditionally. Nothing could stop me from doing exactly that.

This is usually the part of a birth story where people talk about the 3 a.m. drive through snow, the 86-hour labor, or the epidural that didn't work. Not us. By all accounts, Emily's labor was safe and 'normal.' But 'normal' does not mean 'easy.' Hours in, I looked over at her and was stunned by her determination and focus. There are few certainties in life, but one I'll never question: mothers in labor embody the pinnacle of human strength and fortitude. I stand in awe of what those who give birth endure.

I can still place myself in the room on December 6th, 2019, when Ellie arrived. The unrelenting beeps of the hospital monitors. The scent of rubbing alcohol and hospital cafeteria food. A whiteboard checklist that read 'have baby' with a dry-erase smiley beside it. Nurses and doctors rushing in and out. Voices calling out medical terms I didn't understand And then finally, the cry of a newborn cutting through it all. Emily and I locked eyes, whispered "I love you," and then it happened. Suddenly, we were parents.

In an instant, all the preparation I had clung to vanished. Staring at this tiny girl, swaddled in hospital cotton and resting on Emily's chest, I was overcome by a love so fierce it scrambled my thoughts. Love had a face, eyes, and tiny fingers that wrapped around mine. For a moment, the future disappeared. I was paralyzed in the present. We laughed, we cried, and we shook our heads in disbelief. Ellie was here. She was *our* daughter, and she was healthy, radiant, and impossibly perfect.

When it came time to leave, I must have checked the car seat buckles a hundred times. My hands clenched the wheel as I drove at half the speed limit, a line of cars stacking up behind me. Carrying the car seat through the front door, I felt its weight in one hand and the heavier weight of reality in the other. Okay, I thought, we made it. But now what?

Mike Tyson famously said that "Everyone has a plan until they get punched in the face." For new parents, the punch is sleep deprivation. Those first few nights at home blurred into one endless stretch of feeding, changing, rocking, and second-guessing. We grabbed whatever thirty-minute naps we could.

Exhausting as it was, we were growing into our role as parents. We learned the angles, the rhythms, and the tricks. We alternated diaper changes and feedings, bath times and nap times. We learned the perfect way to hold her so that she would quickly fall asleep, or how to tilt the bottle to ease her gas. Through trial, error, and bleary-eyed teamwork, we were doing it. We were surviving newborn parenthood.

One sleepless morning, just a few weeks in, I offered to take the 5 a.m. feeding so that Emily could rest. I lifted Ellie out of her bassinet and gently closed our bedroom door behind me. A soft morning light filtered through the sliding glass doors in our living room, casting a calm, amber glow. Outside, a thin layer of snow covered the ground. I wrapped Ellie in blankets and sat with her clinging tightly to my chest. She blinked up at me until her eyes surrendered to sleep. I was running on empty from the last few days, but I knew Ellie must have been too.

I imagined how overwhelming her world must have been. From darkness into light. Pain, hunger, warmth, confusion all crushing into her for the first time with no way to make sense of it. I wasn't the only one trying to figure out life. From day one, she too was trying to understand it all. And in that moment, I understood: instead of racing years ahead, what she needed most was for me to meet her here, in the present.

In the year that followed, Ellie's personality revealed itself slowly, then all at once. We watched fleeting infant smirks blossom into belly laughs as our wobbly nine month old learned to walk. Her dark newborn hair softened into golden red waves and curls. The crib, once an empty reminder of my fatherhood nerves, was now the place where each night ended with a story and kiss goodnight. Those first nine months held a new, exciting milestone each day, but they were not without their challenges.

In September 2020, after what we expected to be a routine check-up, we learned Ellie would need minor surgery to remove a benign hemangioma above her right ear. A cluster of blood vessels had caused a small protrusion along her upper ear. It was harmless for the moment, but could eventually deform her ear and affect her hearing as she grew. The doctors reassured us: a straightforward procedure, an hour at most, home the same day. With that, we agreed to move forward.

The morning of the surgery, we found ourselves once again in a hospital room filled with high-pitched beeps and cold metal trays. To pass the time, we stacked Ellie's favorite books on the chair beside us. She sat on my lap, giggling as I read *Brown Bear, Brown Bear* for what felt like the hundredth time.

The moment was nightmarishly surreal. Ellie, only ten months old, wore a hospital gown. Her tiny legs kicked against me, her weight warm and heavy in my arms. It was impossible to reconcile her giggles with the sterile smell of antiseptic and the gleam of stainless steel around us. How could innocence and danger sit side by side in the same room?

Around us, the COVID-19 pandemic was still in full force. Nurses and doctors moved quickly through the room with masks on, rubbing sanitizer into their hands as they described what to expect. When it came time to wheel Ellie into surgery, the nurses gently suggested we step out for coffee or some air. We hugged her tightly, kissed her forehead, and let go. I had never felt so helpless as I did walking out of that room.

I rooted myself to a waiting room chair and stared at the clock. Three minutes had passed. I took one bite of a protein bar but nausea kept me from swallowing the rest. Ellie, still not even a year old, was under anesthesia. Somewhere nearby, a surgeon was preparing to place a scalpel against her head. That image gripped my mind and would not let go. *What if something goes wrong?*

Eventually, I stepped outside to clear my head. Hospitals keep the temperature somewhere between frozen tundra and Antarctic winter; I zippered my jacket tighter and began to wander the hall. A toddler in a wheelchair rolled past, pushed slowly by his parents. His casted arm sat stiff at his side, looking strangely out of place against his small frame. How easy it is to forget that toddler bones can break just like adult ones.

Further down the hallway, I passed a sign for Pediatric Oncology. A young girl in a pink dress walked out holding her mother's hand, her light-up sneakers flashing red with each step. Wisps of hair clung to her otherwise bald head. That sight pinned me where I stood. I had been drowning in fear over a benign mass on Ellie's ear, but here were parents carrying an entirely different weight. They were living inside a nightmare I could barely comprehend.

I stood there frozen, watching the red lights from her sneakers light up the hallway as her mother gently guided her forward. That image carved itself into my memory - not because it was tragic, but because it was impossibly normal. A little girl, holding her mother's hand, walking down a hallway like any other child would. Except, of course, she wasn't like any other child. This wasn't normal. My fear for Ellie's surgery collided with something much larger. I had spent the last hour consumed by the thought of a small procedure on her ear. Just steps away, other parents were spending their hours hoping for one more tomorrow.

Back in the waiting room, I hugged Emily tightly and shared what I had seen. The broken arm, the bald little girl, the scalpel on my baby's ear: none of this should be happening. I didn't have answers. I didn't have a framework. All I had was fear, love, and the fragile hope that it would be enough to carry us through the day.

I was spiraling, caught between how I thought the world *should* work and the harsh reality of how it *does* work. This was my first real exposure to the dark side of life's unending questions since my grandpa died. Except now, it felt closer, sharper, impossible to ignore. It wasn't that the framework I dreamt up wasn't working, it was that I hadn't even thought to reach for it. The emotions of the moment left me spinning. I wasn't ready to consider what some philosopher from two thousand years ago might advise.

"Parents of Eleanor Bottone?" A nurses's voice cut through the fog. We leapt to our feet, rushing to the desk before being escorted to see the doctor. Relief washed over me as he explained the surgery had gone exactly as planned. Ellie was resting just a few feet away and we would get to see her soon. A bandage would wrap her head for a few days, but she would make a full recovery within a week. In just a few hours, we would be taking her home.

We walked into the room to find Ellie fast asleep, a hard plastic cup shielding her ear and white bandages wrapped around her tiny head. She stirred for a few minutes, her eyes fluttering open in a mixture of fear and confusion that broke me. She cried, a high panicked wail that felt sharper than any scalpel. We cried with her. Relief, exhaustion, and love filled the room. In that moment, all the fear that had knotted in our chest for hours seemed to unravel. The weight didn't vanish all at once, but it began to lift, leaving the room lighter with every breath she took. Holding her again reminded us that she was still our baby, still the giggly toddler who loved bedtime stories and playing picnic. Now, she carried a scar as a reminder of her strength.

I brushed Ellie's red curls back from the white hospital bandage and secured the car seat buckles. The image of those flashing sneakers lingered in my mind as I kissed her cheek and started the long drive home. I thought about how lucky we were that the worst of Ellie's troubles was a small scar. In that same building, other children would not get to leave so easily. That day, the world hadn't made sense yet. That night, I held tight to the one thing that did.

3
Moments

The moment outside the pediatric oncology wing stayed with me longer than expected. We walked out of the hospital that day with Ellie safe in our arms, the surgery a success and the bandages temporary. But that encounter with the fragility of life cracked something open again. This time, it felt different.

I realized, now more than ever, how precious moments with Ellie were. Though the COVID lockdown was a devastating time for many, it also gave me opportunities as a father that I'll never stop being grateful for. Working from home meant no more rushing to beat the traffic or hoping I'd catch Ellie before bedtime. I lifted her from her crib each morning and tucked her in each night, savoring every moment we had together. I swapped travel mugs of coffee and pantry protein bars for pancakes I could make together with Ellie perched on the counter beside me. Between meetings, I would sneak downstairs to read a book or sit cross-legged at a tea party, eating pretend pastries.

While the world outside our home was unraveling in the chaos of a pandemic, I anchored to what was within our walls. Through the slowness and stillness, a different kind of purpose began to take shape. Not a grand metaphysical mission, but a series of small, deliberate choices. A moment to moment awareness.

The framework I had once been chasing was something universal, profound, airtight. But it began to shrink - not in significance, but in scope. I shifted my attention to what was actually happening in front of me. Not the narrative, not the noise, just the raw texture of each moment as it arrived. From there, I had a choice in how to frame it. I didn't need to decode some hidden cosmic lesson while Ellie poured invisible tea into plastic cups. I just needed to be there with her. Fully.

My questions changed. I was no longer asking myself what my grandiose meaning or purpose would be. Instead, I began asking myself something simpler, more actionable: *what would it look like to make the most out of this moment?*

Making the most of each moment didn't mean I was always the one to benefit. Often, it simply meant giving Ellie a hug when she scraped her knee or stepping in for the bedtime routine when Emily needed a break. These moments weren't dramatic or profound; they were ordinary. And that was the brilliance of it. Ordinary moments happened dozens of times per day. I no longer had to look over the shoulder of the present toward a meaningful future. By being fully present, any anxiety about the future softened. If I could string together enough of these maximized moments, the future would sort itself out.

Of course, what 'making the most out of this moment' looked like wasn't always obvious or easy. Toddler tantrums and long workdays often made presence feel like a moving target. Some days, I just didn't have it in me. But even through the challenges of parenthood, the framing helped. Each moment became its own opportunity: one I could maximize or miss.

That question slowly became a kind of mental habit. Sometimes it meant taking the long way around the park so Ellie could feed the ducks. Other times it meant sipping coffee a little slower before the house woke up. This wasn't some overnight epiphany that I instantly mastered. It also wasn't some Earth-shattering life hack that flipped my world upside down. It was quieter than that, almost imperceptible at first. A slow accumulation of choices, small shifts in how I noticed and responded to the moments right in front of me. One hug instead of a sigh, one deep breath instead of a snap, one pause to listen instead of rushing to the next task. Over time, those little decisions stacked up, and they began to change not just how I experienced fatherhood, but how I experienced life itself.

While Ellie was learning new words, building block towers, and outgrowing her crib, I was trying to grow, too. That meant reshaping my routines, questioning my defaults, and choosing presence again and again.

Over time, my role as a father evolved and became more clear. I wasn't just surviving parenthood; I was curating it. My mission was to find the smallest of opportunities to make the biggest impact in Ellie's life. I found joy in searching for the little sparks that might ignite something in Ellie: a question, a connection, a smile.

In Ellie's smile, I saw pure, immediate, and unfiltered happiness. I also learned more from that smile than I had in any philosophy text. Children have a way of turning the ordinary into something extraordinary. Every experience, no matter how small, is brand new. A cardboard box becomes a rocket ship. A walk through our backyard becomes a safari. There was no search for meaning in our pretend space flight. There was just delight in the now. Ellie's smile was constant reminder that kids already figured out what adults spend their life searching for: happiness in the present.

Paradoxically, in my search for something permanent and certain, I found fulfillment in the fleeting. In those moments, I stopped searching for the *why* of life. I just started living it.

The byproduct of making the most of each moment is the chance to constantly experience and learn something new. It creates a beautiful, self-sustaining cycle: each new experience opened the door to another moment to be maximized, which in turn made space for even more new experiences. Naturally, I began to ask myself a life-changing questions for our family: how can I ensure we are always in a position to experience new things?

The attempts Emily and I made to answer that question always circled back to where we might be best positioned to experience them. Despite living in New Jersey our entire lives, we both shared the same goal: moving out of the increasingly expensive state.

This may come as shocking news, but children are not cheap, especially when combined with COVID-era inflation and an uncertain economy. Our grocery bills quickly doubled after adding diapers and formula. Ellie was growing so fast that it felt like she outgrew her wardrobe monthly. The prospect of our family growing was becoming more real, too. Life wouldn't stop getting more expensive. Yes, we could get by just fine if we kept the budget tight. But did we want to just get by? Is that what would provide our family with the most experiences? If not, what can we do to change our course?

One frigid winter night, Emily and I watched snow pile up from the season's third storm in as many weeks. New Jersey isn't exactly known for its snowfall, but winters can still be brutal. Snowfall totals from a single storm often crept past 12 inches, which usually meant the entire state shut down for a day or two. I dreaded storms like this. Our driveway stretched over 30 yards; that winter alone, I had already spent dozens of hours shoveling the icy mess.

As I stood at the window, watching snowflakes whip sideways under the streetlight, the weight of it all pressed in. It wasn't just the driveway. It was the cost of living, the rhythm of our days, the question of what we were building for Ellie and for our family. Clearing snow felt like the perfect metaphor: no matter how much I shoveled, more would pile on. I couldn't shake the sense that we needed a different foundation, somewhere we weren't always digging ourselves out just to stand still.

Emily and I lay in bed, lights off, when I suggested we should just move to somewhere it never snows.

"Maybe move to the South, spend every day in the sun?" she quipped.

"I'm in if you're in," I half-joked, not quite sure how serious either of us were. I grabbed my phone, opened a house-hunting app, and began scrolling. The houses were cheaper than I expected. Property taxes were a third of what we were paying. And wait - how many sunny days did they get per year?

"You know," I wondered aloud, "the company headquarters is in Charlotte. I could probably keep my job and work right from there."

We volleyed ideas back and forth, inching away from the hypothetical and moving toward something like reality. I flipped on the nightstand lamp and we sat up in bed. For hours that night, we talked about schools, neighborhood, finances, weather, and the experiences that would be waiting for us. Before the lights turned off again, we both knew this wasn't just idle dreaming. We didn't say it out loud, but something inside us had shifted.

By morning, the idea had a momentum of its own. Before Emily even woke up, I had already pulled up more learnings and bookmarked towns across North Carolina that seemed perfect for our family. But alongside that excitement, a harsh reality was setting in about what we would be leaving behind in New Jersey. How often would we get to see our families? What about all the friendships we've made? What if we uprooted everything, only to hate it? Thomas Sowell's maxim replayed in my head: *There are no solutions, only trade offs.*

Those trade offs cut deep. When we finally shared the news with Emily's family, they were understandably devastated. We hated the thought of being further away from them too. But beneath their disappointment was a quiet understanding I will always respect. They knew we weren't running away; we were running toward something. Toward possibility, toward growth, and toward the kind of framework we were only beginning to live by.

The impending move filled us with anticipation and a strange kind of calm, as if the act of choosing our own path had already lightened the weight of the present. But we weren't ready to pack up right away. Though the decision to move was made, we needed time to plan, to prepare, and to wrap our heads around all that was about to change.

The months that followed became a peculiar blend of dreaming and routine. We were still in New Jersey, still shoveling snow, and still squeezing in tea parties between meetings. But everything felt charged with new meaning. Each ordinary moment became something to savor, not just because of what it was, but because of what it pointed toward. We weren't just waiting for a move, we were rehearsing for the life we wanted to live when we got there.

While we planned for a life in North Carolina, the most exciting change wasn't geographic, it was personal. Our family was growing. Rosie James Bottone, Ellie's baby sister, was due in the summer of 2021, and her arrival added a whole new dimension to the path we were on. Our lives were no longer just inching toward change; they were bursting with it in the best way. Emily and I exchanged baby name lists each night. Ellie learned to say "Big Sister" with uncontainable pride. Our dinner conversations blurred together with talk of strollers and mortgage rates, swaddles and school zones. For the first time in a long while, it felt like everything was coming together.

Rosie arrived on a hot August morning, the kind of morning where the air feels heavy before the sun fully rises. I remember the blast of hospital air conditioning hitting my face when we walked in. We were nervous, but it felt nothing like Ellie's birth. We considered ourselves seasoned parents. Calm, prepared, present.

When Rosie finally entered the world, it was as if the whole room paused. Her first, fierce cry broke through the stillness and in an instant, we were a family of four. She was impossibly light in my arms, so different from the toddler-sized hugs I was used to from Ellie. The nurse said she was healthy and strong; I remember nodding along, but getting lost in Rosie's eyes whenever they'd flutter open. The blueish, grey hue looked just like Emily's eyes: they were mesmerizing.

Later that night, after the visitors left and the room fell quiet, I sat besides Rosie's bassinet. Her tiny chest gently rose and fell as she slept. I thought about how much of her story hadn't been written yet. I wondered how different she might be from Ellie. I thought a lot about myself as a father; these past two years had changed me. After Ellie's birth, I left the hospital hoping I wouldn't mess anything up. With Rosie's arrival, I felt ready to take on whatever life could throw at me. I didn't know what challenges would come or how things would unfold, but I did know this: Emily and I would face it together.

At least, that's what we told ourselves. The fundamental flaw that parents fall for when having a second child is assuming that experience guarantees predictability. That what worked once will work again. Quickly, our confidence gave way to exhaustion.

Rosie had her own script. She wouldn't sleep, struggled with feedings, and cried through painful reflux. Nap times were unpredictable at best, non-existent at worst. Just like that, we were no longer the seasoned parents we thought we were. We were beginners again, navigating this new environment with no familiar tools.

Days blurred into weeks, and weeks into months. For the better part of Rosie's first year, Emily and I each woke up multiple times each night to soothe her. Many mornings, I showed up to work after just two or three hours of broken sleep, only to repeat the same cycle again later that night. There's a reason sleep deprivation is classified as form of torture. I was physically drained, mentally foggy, and emotionally shattered.

The mind-bending confusion of it all was that I was happiest when I was with Rosie or Ellie. Parenthood is strange and astonishing in that way. Even under the crushing weight of stress and exhaustion, there was always time for bedtime stories, duck duck goose, or our nightly living room dance parties. Even when Rosie's cries jolted me awake at 3 a.m. for the third time that night, there was something about holding her close in the quiet darkness that I actually looked forward to. With her head resting on my chest, the stress seemed to dissolve, if only for a few minutes.

Through those sleepless nights, the move to North Carolina was never far from our minds. In fact, it became something of a mental lighthouse; it was distant, but steady. It offered a horizon to look forward to beyond the haze of midnight feedings and diaper changes.

As Rosie began to settle in to a reliable rhythm and Ellie adjusted to her role as big sister, our plans for the big move started to crystallize. By the summer of 2022, what had once felt like a wild idea on a snowy night was now within reach. We weren't just scrolling through real estate listings anymore; we were scheduling virtual tours, running numbers with banks, and comparing neighborhoods. If North Carolina was our lighthouse, we were preparing for landfall.

By the time Rosie's first birthday rolled around in August, there were cardboard boxes stacked in nearly every corner of our house. A few weeks later, our offer was accepted on what we could only call our dream home. We weren't just moving to a new house, we were moving on to the next, brightest chapter of our lives. It was shaped by everything we had learned, all we had endured, and everything we were ready to embrace. These past two years had been hectic and exhausting, but the future was just around the corner, and it felt like possibility itself was waiting on the other side.

4
The Call

In the weeks leading up to the move, every familiar routine took on a kind of soft finality. The last strolls around the neighborhood. The last dinners with nearby friends. The last tea parties in the playroom where Ellie had taken her first wobbly steps. There was excitement, sure, but it mingled with the nerves that accompany any massive life change. Were we really about to leave everything behind and start over again, a thousand miles away from anyone we knew?

Those pre-move jitters rippled through our house, growing louder by the day. Even the girls seemed to pick up on the energy. Rosie, after finally settling into something like a rhythm, slipped into another sleep regression that left Emily and me running on fumes. Ellie, usually upbeat and bubbly, seemed off in ways we couldn't ignore.

In the final two weeks before the move, Ellie lost her appetite and barely touched her meals. She spent hours curled up on the couch, uninterested in building block towers or dancing through our kitchen like we used to. For the first time in her life, she had trouble sleeping, waking on two separate nights to complain of stomach pains.

With a week to go before the big move, we decided to bring Ellie to the doctor. Maybe it was a stomach bug? The flu? We hoped it was something we could treat quickly before everything got turned upside down with the move.

The doctor listened carefully and then reassured us: this was likely pre-move anxiety. She explained that Ellie's emotional stress had snowballed into physical symptoms. Her lack of appetite was leading to stomach discomfort and fatigue. It all made sense. She had been asking endless questions about the move, trying in her own way to process the shift we were all feeling. Maybe this was just how her little body was carrying the stress of it all.

When we got home, we sat down with Ellie and painted a picture of what was waiting for her. We showed her photos of the playgrounds near our new house, the community pool with its waterslide and splash pad, and the school less than a mile away. We told her about the friends she would make, the adventures still ahead, and the new places waiting to be discovered.

Over the next few days, her energy seemed to lift. We brought her to the local park and watched her run and laugh with other kids. Her appetite wasn't fully back, but she did seem to be eating more. It was late October and Halloween was right around the corner, too. Ellie woke up each day excitedly asking if it was time to trick-or-treat yet. From our perspective, she was adjusting. Nervous, yes, but steadily warming up to the idea of starting fresh.

While Ellie's mood improved, mine was less settled. The logistics of the move loomed large, leaving plenty of room for doubt. I would drive down to Charlotte on my own, the car packed with our most valuable belongings. I would arrive the night of Monday, October 31st and we could close on the house Tuesday, November 1st. That same day, I'd meet the movers at our new address. For the next few days, I'd unpack most essentials, rebuild Rosie's crib, and get the house baby-ready. Then, that weekend, Emily would make the trip with the girls, officially beginning our new chapter. My parents graciously offered to come with us and stay the first week to help us adjust to life in North Carolina.

We had a plan, a timeline, and a vision. But beneath it all, there was a quiet unease. I couldn't name it yet, but soon it would sharpen into something undeniable.

Chaos struck during my drive down to Charlotte. I had imagined a quiet, reflective trip. This was supposed to be the one final moment of calm before everything changed. Instead, I spent nearly half of the nine-hour drive on the phone with lawyers and real estate agents. The buyers of our home in New Jersey were getting cold feet. On the morning of what was supposed to be our closing day, they blindsided us with last-minute demands we hadn't previously agreed to. I was assured it would get sorted out, but our closing would be delayed at least a day.

That seemingly harmless 24 hour delay sent a grenade through our already delicate timeline. When I finally pulled into the hotel that night, I was a mess of stress and scrambling. I made frantic calls to the movers, utility companies, contractors, and family back home. Everything we had meticulously planned was now shattered to pieces; every last detail needed to be rescheduled. I had pictured arriving in North Carolina to sunshine and structure. Instead,

I had arrived in the middle of a storm whose full force hadn't yet revealed itself.

Back home, Emily was busy trick-or-treating with the girls. Ellie and Rosie were so excited for this night, and I was devastated that I couldn't be with them. Normally, I take pride in never missing the big moments. Holidays, school plays, soccer games - no matter what's going on - I'm there. Always. But this Halloween, the universe had other plans. I hated that I wasn't there.

I waited for the photos and stories with aching anticipation, hoping they might soften the weight of the day. I wanted to see Ellie in her princess costume, Rosie sneaking chocolate before bed. Instead, Emily called me and her voice carried an edge of worry.

Ellie hadn't been herself that night. Despite asking every day for the past month if it was finally time to trick-or-treat, she refused to leave the house when the moment came. Even after Emily finally coaxed her into the stroller wagon, Ellie wouldn't ring doorbells or collect candy. The pictures told the rest of the story. Ellie looked pale and drained, her costume hanging loose around her shoulders, her eyes heavy with exhaustion.

Maybe she was upset that I wasn't there. Maybe hearing I had arrived in North Carolina made the move feel real and scary all over again. It seemed possible that's all this was. But deep down, we knew something was off. The next morning, Emily called the pediatrician. She wanted Ellie seen.

On Tuesday morning, I learned our closing was delayed yet again, this time until Wednesday. I spent the morning running another gauntlet of phone calls, trying to keep everyone updated and the plan from collapsing.

Then, early that afternoon, Emily called. The pediatrician's office had lost power, so they were being rerouted across town to another clinic. Still, she insisted it was worth the trip. Ellie hadn't slept much the night before and now looked even more pale and lethargic. When I video called to wish them luck at the appointment, I barely recognized Ellie. Her face was sunken, her eyes dull. My stomach sank.

Surely, this was a nasty flu or maybe mononucleosis. I remembered an outbreak of mono in high school and the symptoms lined up. I told Emily as much and we said our goodbyes, clinging to that theory like a lifeline.

An hour later, my phone rang again.

For the first few seconds, all I could hear was the rush of wind and the hurried shuffle of footsteps. A strange calm washed over me. I glanced at the clock. Ellie's appointment had only started ten minutes ago. The doctor must have made a quick diagnosis. It was probably something viral, something treatable. Emily would say Ellie just needed rest, maybe a prescription, and I'd see them in North Carolina by the weekend.

Then Emily's voice came through. It was shaky, like she was working hard just to hold it steady.

"Hi. Don't be scared. Everything's going to be okay," she began. Then, a pause. "The doctor said Ellie either has a viral infection… or she may…" She trailed off.

"She may, what?" My chest tightened, already bracing.

"The doctor said her symptoms may point to a form of cancer. I'm on my way to the emergency room now. My parents are meeting us there."

I was paralyzed. It was like being punched in the gut by something you didn't know could even hit you. Cancer? No. That wasn't on the table. She's not even three years old. Toddlers don't get cancer. That's not how life works. The pediatrician had to be mistaken. This wasn't real.

"Okay," I managed. "Please keep me updated."

I hung up. Silence filled the hotel room. My heart pounded slow but loud, each thud ricocheting inside of my ribs. I stumbled into the desk chair, dizzy, whispering to myself that cancer was only a worst-case scenario. It would be ruled out shortly after Emily arrived at the ER. It had to be.

This move to North Carolina was supposed to be our reset. My early arrival, the packed car, and the meticulously planned closing was all proof that a stable life was finally within reach. And yet here I was: in a cheap hotel room, a thousand miles away from family, while Emily endured the most traumatic day of her life without me. My daughters needed me. My family needed me. And I wasn't there.

I closed my eyes. Breathed deep. Tried to remember the framework. *Stay present. Focus on what's in front of you. What can you do, right now, to move things forward? What would it look like to make the most out of this moment?*

I called our real estate agent and hastily explained the situation, stumbling through words. I explained that I planned to fly back home and be at the hospital with Emily and Ellie. But as I said it out loud, I realized I was describing something I couldn't actually do. It wasn't that simple.

If I left, I would miss the closing on our new home. We had already delayed closing twice and the sellers were getting nervous. If I wasn't there in person, they could walk away. If they did, we'd have no home. And my car, packed with our most valuable belongings? Movers? Utilities? Baby-proofing? Every detail unraveled all at once.

Answers. That's what I needed. Not philosophy. Not breath-work. Answers.

By nighttime, I still hadn't eaten. My stomach was a tangle of nerves and nausea. Eventually, I forced down a few bites of takeout under the dim light of the desk lamp. The food was dry, tasteless. I pushed it aside.

Emily's updates slowed to almost nothing. Every hour was the same. *Still waiting for tests.* Then silence.

At 8 p.m., another sound intruded. It was a faint thumping, growing louder with each minute. Then laughter. Footsteps. A door slammed. Music. Some forgettable pop song pulsing through the drywall.

A party. On a Tuesday night.

After the longest, most brutal day of my life…this.

I sat in the dark, waiting for a doctor's verdict on whether my daughter had cancer, while faceless strangers sang along to a song I didn't know.

I closed my eyes, trying to block it out. Sleep was impossible. Answers felt farther still.

I started searching online for what virus Ellie might have. Brief flashes of hope flickered across my screen. Words like "antiviral medications are typically prescribed and patients can be cured in 1 to 2 weeks." Surely, that's all this was. This was Ellie. She would be in her new room playing with her favorite toys in a matter of days.

Suddenly, the vibration of my phone jolted me upright. Emily's photo filled the screen. My pulse quickened as I answered the call.

"Okay, what is it?" I asked, my voice sharper than I meant.

There was no immediate reply. Just silence. A long, awful silence.

And in that silence, I knew.

Every hypothetical, every nightmare, every parent's worst fear - they all lived in that gap. The void between my question and what came next was where life split cleanly in two: before and after this moment.

When Emily finally spoke, her voice was fragile. "I'm going to put the doctor on the phone."

"No. Emily, no," I begged, my voice breaking. "Please tell me she doesn't…"

"Ellie has cancer."

The words shattered me.

I screamed. My body convulsed in a way I'd never felt before. A storm of fear, rage, disbelief, and guilt crashed over me all at once. I couldn't speak. I remember screaming "no" over and over as the phone slipped from my hands landed facedown on the bed.

I couldn't breathe.

Despite crying only a handful of times in my entire life, I was now sobbing uncontrollably, tears pouring like a faucet I couldn't shut off. My chest heaved as I gasped for air. I looked around the hotel room helplessly. It was sterile, impersonal, unfamiliar and I wanted to escape this place. I didn't want to be here. I needed to get out. I need to be with Ellie. *Now.*

"Emily, how?" I managed. "Why is this happening? What are we supposed to do?"

I have always prided myself on being rational, logical, measured. But that part of me was gone, overtaken by something primal. I was spiraling, firing questions into the phone between heaving sobs, desperate for something to make this make sense.

Under it all, the guilt was deafening. Louder than the music next door. Louder than the sobs. I was a thousand miles away. My family was living the darkest moment of their lives, and I wasn't there.

"I...I need to let the doctor explain," Emily said softly. "I can't...I can't do it."

The the doctor's came through, clinical and detached. He listed tests, blood cell counts, preliminary scans. I tried to follow, but it all blurred into the static of medical jargon.

"We can say with certainty that you daughter has a form of cancer," he concluded, "but at this point we're still waiting to determine whether it's leukemia or lymphoma. We'll know more in the coming hours."

That was it.

No *I'm sorry.*

No *She's going to be okay.*

Just the cold finality of his diagnosis.

Anger rose in my throat. This was my daughter. The most precious thing on this Earth. She was perfect. She *is* perfect. And this stranger just handed me the worst news a parent can hear as if he were reading the weather report.

"Please put my wife on the phone." I responded, my words low and firm. A shuffle, then Emily's tearful breath.

"Emily, listen to me. She's going to be okay. We're going to get through this. She *has* to be okay."

"I know, I know," she whispered, pulling herself together. "I know."

"I'm going to come there. I'm going to hang up this call right now and finding the fastest way to get home. Please call me the second the test results come in. I love you."

"I love you too."

The call ended and the room filled once more with the thumping bass of the music next door. I tried to steady my breathing, tried to focus on anything but the nightmare unfolding. I stood to walk to the bathroom, but the dizziness overtook me. I stumbled forward, barely making it in time to vomit up what little food I'd forced down earlier.

From the other side of the wall came the soundtrack of someone else's Tuesday night: carefree laughter, pulsing music, memories being created. Just inches away, life was effortless and light. On my side of the wall, life was coming undone.

The contrast felt cruel. It amplified the injustice I was already choking on. *She is not even three years old,* I kept thinking. *This isn't supposed to happen.*

None of the Stoics prepared me for this. None of their tidy aphorisms made my daughter's diagnosis any less real. I had built a philosophy around being present, anchored in the moment. But now, all I wanted was to escape it.

And then another realization crept in: I would have to share the news. I would have to *say* it out loud. To my sister. To my parents. I would have to say the words 'Ellie has cancer.' I would be the one to deliver *their* before and after.

I sat on the edge of the bed, phone gripped tightly in my hand, paralyzed. I knew what I had to do. I just couldn't do it yet.

My mind drifted.

I thought of Ernest Shackleton. In Alfred Lansing's *Endurance*, Shackleton's ill-fated 1915 expedition to cross Antarctica ends before it even begins. His ship becomes trapped in pack ice in the Waddell Sea before reaching the continent. Despite the odds, not a single crew member perished. For nearly two years, they survived on ice floes, makeshift camps, and fragments of hope.

What struck me most wasn't just the survival but the accounts from the men themselves. The crew's journals brimmed with faith in their leader. Even in the most harrowing circumstances, they wrote of trust, confidence, and admiration of their leader. They spoke of his bravery, optimism, and leadership in the most dire of situations. He was unshakable.

Shackleton's own journal told another story. Lansing writes that "[Shackleton] suffered an almost pathological dread of losing control of the situation" and that "of all their enemies - the cold, the ice, the sea - he feared none more than demoralization."

His fear wasn't the ice or the wild animals or even starvation. The true threat was the morale unraveling and belief eroding. Shackleton's greatness wasn't in being fearless; it was in being afraid and still choosing to lead.

The fear of failure, of loss of control, and of losing hope were all set aside in an unwavering commitment to push forward and survive another day. "Difficulties," he writes, "are just things to overcome, after all."

Sitting on that sagging hotel bed, I realized that I had a choice. As my world crumbled around me, I could choose to crumble with it. Or I could rise. I could carry hope where my search for certainty had failed. I could be steady, unbroken, even when afraid. It was my choice.

This wasn't the blind, flimsy hope of naive optimism; it was the hard earned, battle tested kind that comes from choosing to endure. Endurance is a decision, not an instinct. When the body is frozen with fear, the mind must take the first step. Soon, those around me would either see me paralyzed, or see me move.

Now, making the most of this moment meant doing the hardest thing: stepping forward, even without knowing where the step would lead. Even if it was only making a phone call, putting on a mask of confidence, and assurance I didn't feel yet.

As I dialed the number, preparing to speak the words no parent ever wants to say, I thought of Shackleton. Not the man in the legend, but the man in the cold. Afraid. Alone. Unsure. But still leading. Despite the gravest of circumstances, I couldn't let my family lose hope.

With each call, the diagnosis became more real. Saying the word out loud - "cancer" - felt misplaced, like it didn't belong in our story. But there it was. And I knew that by speaking it, I wasn't just informing people, I was dragging them into the nightmare with me.

It had been no more than an hour since I'd gotten the call from Emily. In those sixty minutes, I aged a decade. I heard the cries from friend and relatives, relayed all the unknowns still ahead, and promised call backs when I learned more. Those conversations changed me. I wasn't just someone's

46

son, cousin, or friend. With each call, I felt myself becoming *the cancer parent*. It happened in real time, in the pity of their voice or the tone of the text messages that came flooding in. The identity consumed me like an outfit I never asked to wear. I'd come to understand later that it's an identity I would never fully lose.

I drifted in and out of sleep, never for more than thirty minutes at a time. It was the longest night of my life. But now the sun crept in through the wide hotel windows. Overnight, Emily shared a small mercy: Ellie finally slept through the night. Despite the pokes and prods of constant vitals checks, the medications and IV fluids had brought some temporary relief.

It was time to carve out order in the chaos. Flights to New Jersey left later that morning. If I was quick, I could close on the house then catch a flight back to be with Ellie. I called our real estate agent, clinging to the idea that doing something might get us back in control.

The cosmos had other ideas.

The closing was delayed yet again. This time, they promised it was final. What was delivered to me as 'great news, you are finally closing' was, in reality, just more disorder. More calls to contractors. More rescheduled movers. More delay. And worst of all, more time away from Ellie. I couldn't stay, but I couldn't leave. If I boarded a plane now, we'd lose the house. With the sale of our New Jersey home already finalized, we'd have no where to go.

I started a video call with Emily, unprepared for what came next.

Ellie's face appeared on the screen. Even in this madness, she was beautiful. The hospital gown laid loose on her small shoulders. Medical tubes trailed down her arm. Her head rested gently on the pillow. She looked frail. Tired. And yet, through it all, there was a flicker of light in her eyes when she saw me.

"Hi Daddy," she said.

I was already holding back tears.

Her voice. That sweet voice I had heard a million times before while singing, playing, or asking for one more bedtime story. It was innocent, kind, and utterly unaware of the nightmare she was at the center of. Until now, I had never spent more than a single day away from Ellie. In that moment, I wanted to crawl through the phone and wrap her in my arms. I wanted to trade places, to take the cancer in her blood and put it in mine instead.

"Hi Ellie," I managed. I needed to stay strong. *She cannot see me cry*, I thought. I repeated it in my head a thousand times, desperate to hold it together.

"I'm at the hospital," she said. "Mommy said I'm a little sick. Are you going to come see me?"

Tears welled in my eyes. I measured each breath, steadying my voice.

"Daddy's going to be with you really soon," I said. "I love you so much."

"I love you too, Daddy"

Emily stepped into frame just as the tears began to fall to my face. I explained the closing situation and felt the weight shift in both of our rooms. We didn't need to say it. We both knew what had to be done. I would stay in North Carolina one more day, close on the house, and immediately head back to New Jersey. If I didn't stay, we'd lose the home. We'd lose any semblance of positivity, of progress, of hope.

I had seen what I thought to be the absolute apex of strength and determination when Emily gave birth to Ellie and Rosie. My admiration, love, and respect for her had only deepened throughout our marriage. But this was different. On that call, I watched her step into a new identity; it was one she never asked for either. She, too, had become a cancer parent.

There was an unspoken bond that formed between us in that moment, one somehow even deeper than the marriage we already shared. We were the only two people in the world who truly knew what the other was feeling. There was a strange comfort in that, a lifeline in the middle of a storm I wouldn't wish on anyone.

I wasn't going through this alone. Not with Emily at my side.

But even with that anchor, the storm was just beginning. The past 24 hours pressed down on me like a weight I couldn't shake. I hadn't eaten, hadn't slept, hadn't done anything besides try to survive one minute at a time.

I drove to a grocery store near the hotel to grab some snacks for the room and the trip home the next day. A glowing sign in the window advertised that night's lottery prize in bold neon, as if hope could be bought for a few dollars. Inside, it was just another quiet Wednesday afternoon.

I wandered the aisles without purpose, scanning shelves but not really seeing them. I just needed something, anything, to pull me out of my own head. Every stranger that passed and offered a polite nod added to a quiet, growing tension inside me. Part of me clung to that kindness, reminded of how fragile life is, how invisible most burdens really are. Another part of me, raw and aching, envied each passerby. They were planning dinner. I was clawing through hell.

At checkout, the cashier smiled as I unloaded my cart onto the conveyor belt. I managed a smile back, thin and automatic. For a moment, I was back in another checkout line years earlier, after my grandfather died.

"You playing that lotto tonight?" she asked.

"No, not me," I replied flatly, "You?"

"Oh yessir," she started, "That many million? All my problems?" she waved a hand in the air, "Poof, gone."

I let out an audible laugh for the first time in days. I didn't know what else to do. The irony hit me hard. *Not all my problems,* I wanted to say.

I wanted to tell her everything. To ask how money could cure the cancer inside my daughter's blood. To tell her that the lottery wasn't the answer she was looking for. That she should hold tight to what she already had. That she should be grateful she wasn't me, wasn't my daughter. But I said nothing. The *beep, beep,* of each item scanned across the counter filled the silence, echoing the machines at Ellie's hospital bed.

"You enjoy the rest of your day," she said, handing me the receipt.

"Thanks," I said, and smiled again. A real one, maybe. Or close enough.

I stepped out of the grocery store with a small bag in one hand and a receipt I hadn't meant to take. The sky was beginning to dim, the last light of day stretching thin across the parking lot. Somewhere behind me, the cashier was probably making small talk about the lottery to the next customer, oblivious to the storm that just passed her by.

On the drive back to the hotel, I replayed that moment again and again. Maybe it was her easy smile, maybe the joke about a ticket erasing all her problems. I had been seconds away from snapping, from telling her what *real* problems looked like.

But I didn't.

As I pulled into those hotel lot, I was glad had I hadn't. She didn't deserve my bitterness, even if it masqueraded as truth. She had been kind. She had no idea. None of them did. And that wasn't their fault.

What I realized was this: the world was still turning. People were still shopping for dinner, picking up lottery tickets and asking strangers how their day was. I could let that contrast harden me, or I could let it remind me of what I was fighting for. Normal. Ordinary. Uneventful days.

I wasn't better than my anger yet, but I wanted to be. I wanted to be someone Ellie or Rosie would see someday and say *that's what strong looks like*. I wanted to be someone anyone could look at and see endurance.

I walked into the hotel room not looking for pity, escape, or empathy. I had made it through another day and for right now, that was enough. The next one was already on its way. But there was one last phone call I needed to take.

5
Our New Home

Ellie was diagnosed with leukemia on November 2nd, 2022. That night, still in a hotel room half a country away, I joined a call with Emily and the team of doctors caring for Ellie. When the official diagnosis arrived, it was strangely comforting. Yesterday, it was an unnamed shadow - just "cancer." Today, it had a name: B-Cell Acute Lymphoblastic Leukemia (ALL).

The comfort didn't come from the label itself, but from the doctors' clarity. They weren't guessing. They had a plan. It was treatable; it was curable. I didn't know what B-cell ALL was, but I knew one thing: we would beat it.

B-Cell Acute Lymphoblastic Leukemia is a cancer of the blood and bone marrow. In this disease, the bone marrow produces too many immature white blood cells. These abnormal cells don't die: they multiply. This crowds out the healthy cells the body needs to survive.

Suddenly, Ellie's symptoms made sense. The fatigue. The paleness. The stomach pains. They were the quiet warnings of a body overwhelmed by those abnormal cells. Her hemoglobin levels were dangerously low. She was severely anemic, likely dizzy and aching for days, and far too young to put her suffering into words. The thought of my daughter suffering in silence wrecked me as much as the diagnosis itself.

We learned that B-Cell ALL is the most common form of leukemia in children, accounting for nearly 80% of all cases. About 2,400 children are diagnosed in the US each year. But common didn't mean simple. The National Cancer Institute classifies cases as 'High Risk' if the white blood cell count exceeds 50,000 at diagnosis.

Ellie's was over 80,000.

Even so, the prognosis was encouraging. More than 85% of children under the aged of 18 who follow the treatment plan become long-term survivors. The doctors said this to reassure us, and it did. But a parent, it was impossible not to hear the number we didn't speak about. The other 15%.

Treatment would span two and a half years. That meant Ellie would spend her third, fourth, and fifth birthdays in the grip of chemotherapy. Some days it would mean anesthesia and surgical procedures at the hospital. Others would require daily medications or injections Ellie would take at home. It would be our responsibility to measure out the oral medications or prepare the needles for injections. We were parents turned caregivers.

Most of her treatments would be administered through a port surgically implanted just above her heart, a direct line into the major vein for blood draws, chemo infusions, and transfusions. Every step of treatment was broken into phases. Each phase came with its own rules: where she could go, who she could see, what risks we needed to watch for, what side effects might come.

The first phase, Induction, would begin immediately. For the next 30 days, our lives would shrink to a single hospital room in the Pediatric Oncology Unit in a New Brunswick, NJ hospital. It was two hundred square feet. Every meal, every night's sleep, every family moment would be contained within those walls.

Our 'Day 1' was the same day we originally expected to move into our new home in North Carolina. Instead of unpacking boxes, we were unpacking the reality of cancer.

The goal of Induction was to eliminate visible signs of leukemia and allow healthy blood cells to grow again. But leukemia cells are notoriously stubborn, hiding throughout the body. Doctors told us Ellie would look healthier by the end of the first month, but it would take 30 more months of treatment to ensure the cancer didn't return.

I sat at the hotel room desk, scribbling notes into a tiny notepad by the phone. I didn't understand everything the doctors said, but I felt the conviction in their voices. They didn't sugarcoat the road ahead. It would be long and difficult, but there was a plan.

And according to that plan, Ellie would beat this.

Still, I couldn't stop asking the questions that haunted me: how did we get here? What invisible threat had pulled cancer into our lives? Was it something we fed her? Something we did wrong in infancy? Some cruel accident of biology?

Doctors explained that leukemia begins when a chromosome is damaged, disrupting the normal process of blood cell development. But critically, no one knows why that damage occurs. Not really. Research is ongoing. Maybe one day we'll understand how to prevent it. But for now, the answer was as unsatisfying as it was unchangeable: randomness.

There it was, again: randomness. The same force that took my grandfather. The same force that eventually touches all of us, no matter how carefully we live or how desperately we try to outrun it. The body performs billions upon billions of biological functions each day and not all of them go right. Most of us roll perfect sevens over and over again without ever realizing how lucky we are. We mistake consistency for immunity. But no one outruns the odds forever. The house always wins.

Still, we reach for meaning. As humans, we are wired to find signal in the noise, to chase purpose through pain. But in this case, there was no greater plan, no moral test, no karmic debt. Just a random, catastrophic biological error that entered Ellie's bloodstream.

As Christopher Hitchens once wrote, "To the dumb question 'Why me?' The cosmos barely bothers to return the reply: 'Why not?'"

Asking why was a dead end. It was a spiral with no answer at the bottom. Eventually, my mental framework began to reassemble. What is in my control now? What's the best use of my energy? I have this moment: what will I do, right now, to help Ellie?

Those thoughts distilled into a simple mantra: "This is happening: now what?"

We had received life-altering news, but that didn't change our duty. Out situation was not what we had imagined, but the question was no longer *why*. It was, *what's next?*

For me, the next step was getting to the hospital. I needed to be with Ellie. Her port surgery was scheduled for November 4th, the day after our scheduled closing. I would not miss it. Since we'd be living in the hospital for the next month, I decided to drive the full eight hours to New Jersey with most our most essential belongings.

On the morning of November 3rd, I arrived at the lawyer's office, signed the closing documents in record time, and hit the road. As the miles stretched ahead of me, I searched for something to steady my mind. I opened the audiobook of *Meditations* by Marcus Aurelius, a familiar companion in moments of strain.

"Everything that happens is either endurable or not. If it's endurable, then endure it. Stop complaining." Aurelius wrote, "If it's unendurable…then stop complaining. Your destruction will mean its end as well." (*Meditations, 10.3*)

I had heard these lines dozens of times before. It was a cornerstone of Stoic thought: rational courage, composure, acceptance in the face of hardship. But until now, it had always been hypothetical. A bit of ancient wisdom, useful in theory.

Now, I was living it.

Leukemia was our new reality. No amount of anger or grief could erase the diagnosis. No complaining or pity could soften the road ahead.

If it's endurable, then endure it.

That's where Aurelius' brilliances lives. Not just in the idea of endurance, but the implied choice within. We didn't choose this storm, but we could choose how we would face it.

We could collapse under its weight. No one would blame us. We were parents of a child with cancer. Breaking down would be understandable. Acceptable.

Or, we could endure.

We could make the decision, however impossible it seemed, to stand firm. To show up fully, clear-eyed and steady, for Ellie, for each other, and for whatever came next. Not because we felt brave, but because there was no other choice. Because Ellie needed us to.

With each passing highway sign, I felt the grip of uncertainty tighten, then loosen, then shift into something else: resolve.

When I finally pulled into the hospital parking lot, I sat in silence. On the other side of those walls was a new life. It was one my family had already begun living, and one I had only witnessed from a distance.

I stepped out of the car and walked toward the entrance. It was time to face it. It was time to endure.

The Pediatric Oncology Unit felt surreal, each detail a contradiction. Crayons stacked on top of medical equipment. Bicycles with training wheels resting beside IV poles. Brightly colored drawings taped beside room numbers. My mind flashed back to the blinking red lights on the shoes of the girl I saw walk out of these doors two years ago. I never imagined I'd be walking through them myself.

And then I heard it. A giggle. Ellie's voice.

I ran toward it.

There she was, my beautiful Ellie. Sitting on a hospital bed, a wristband loose around her thin wrist, an IV in her arm. Her smile was a life raft in the storm that consumed the last week. I held back tears as I wrapped my arms around her and squeezed tight. I stayed there for what felt like an eternity. I couldn't let go.

"I missed you, Daddy!"

"I missed you too, Ellie."

Then, Emily. If there was ever a measure of what we can endure, Emily had already surpassed it. We didn't need words; our embrace said it all. Whatever journey awaited us, we'd travel it together. We were terrified, angry, still very much in shock. But we were sure of one thing: we would beat this.

Rosie's absence left a gap in the room. From the day she was born, Rosie had felt every human emotion to its maximum. When she was frustrated or upset, the world knew it. But when she was happy, her joy could brighten the darkest of days. I missed her laugh. I missed the way her tiny arms barely reached around my chest when she hugged me.

No children apart from those being treated were allowed in the oncology unit. Rosie would alternate weeks with my parents and Emily's parents. For this, I was deeply grateful. Surviving cancer, they say, takes a village. Ours was a formidable one, eager to step in wherever necessary.

Since the diagnosis, the gravity of our situation rippled outward. Family and friends reached out in waves, sharing disbelief, sorrow, and love. Some messages were short and simple. Others were long, tearful, spilling over with empathy. Each one chipped away that the illusion that we were in this alone.

And yet, no one, not even those who loved us most, could fully grasp what it meant to hold your child's diagnosis in your hands.

But that's the thing about support. It doesn't require full understanding. It's not always about knowing the right thing to say or being able to take the pain away. Sometimes it's just the presence of another person reminding you that you don't have to carry it alone.

Still, not everyone showed up.

As the news spread, a more painful truth emerged: some friends and family disappeared. A few never reached out. Others offered a single message and never followed up. There were people I thought would be our anchors in the storm. Friends we celebrated with and family we shared holidays and birthdays with were now distant, unsure, or simply absent.

At first, I was confused. Then I was hurt. Eventually, I understood: most people don't know what to do with someone else's pain. They don't know what to say to a parent whose child has cancer, so they say nothing. Not because they don't care, but because they're afraid of saying the wrong thing. Or maybe because our situation was an unwelcome reminder that tragedy could strike anyone. Even them. So they withdrew. They stayed silent. As if distance could protect them from the fragility that our family could no longer ignore.

Grief and fear have a way of rearranging life's cast of characters like that. Some step off stage. Others step forward and surprise you. It's a truth I would come to understand deeply over Ellie's 30 months of treatment.

Tragedy reveals who people are. It revealed us, too. I felt the full weight of that in our first night at the hospital. That night, in a dark hospital room, I saw how easily a person can fall short of who they want to be when life is at its worst.

The room we'd call home for the next 29 nights was half the size of the spare bedroom in our future North Carolina house. Ellie's hospital bed swallowed most of that space. A weathered recliner sat in the corner, a narrow couch pressed against the window. We were grateful to have our bathroom, but the shower stall was so small my shoulders barely fit inside.

We decided Emily would take the couch and I would sleep upright in the recliner. After the nearly all-day drive back to New Jersey, I was wrecked and desperate for rest.

But rest didn't come easily. Nurses entered the room every hour or two to take Ellie's vitals and administer medication. Pediatric oncology nurses perform some of the most demanding, difficult work in the world. I will be forever grateful for the support, love, and care they gave to Ellie throughout her treatment.

That first night, though, I couldn't find it in myself to feel grateful. Ellie finally closed her eyes just before midnight. Between the physical pain and the constant poking and prodding, she desperately needed sleep. I watched her chest rise and fall and wondered what was going through her mind. Days ago, she had been talking about what costume she wanted to wear for Halloween. Now, vials of blood had been pulled from her arm as doctors rushed to stabilize her fragile body.

The soft, red curls of her hair rose and fell with each breath. From the day she was born, Ellie had a full head of hair that seemed to double in size every night. Whenever we walked through town, strangers would stop to marvel at it, offering smiles and compliments about how beautiful it was.

I couldn't stop thinking about how it would be gone soon.

But I told myself to stop thinking about tomorrow. The most important thing I could do for Ellie was focus on today. I needed too zoom in on the here and now. And tonight, she was finally going to get some sleep.

The nurse on duty that night was relatively new. Each time she entered the room, she turned on the overhead lights and bellowed an uninvited, cheerful 'Hello!'

I hated her for it. I hated how easily she flooded the room with light, how little she seemed to notice. Each time, Ellie stirred awake. She barely had time to drift off before being jolted up again, crying softly. By daybreak, she hadn't slept more than a few minutes at a time.

On the nurse's final visit, I snapped.

"Can you PLEASE be more quiet when you come in here? Our daughter has leukemia. She NEEDS sleep." I said sternly.

The words were out before I could stop them. The instant they landed, I regretted them.

I looked into the nurse's eyes and saw everything: fear, remorse, exhaustion. Later, I would learn she had just started night shifts. Fresh out of medical school, she was working thankless hours and taking vitals from critically ill children…only to be yelled at by a tired, scared father.

She didn't deserve it.

Socrates once said "No one errs or does wrong willingly or knowingly." I believe that. The nurse wasn't trying to wake Ellie. She wasn't careless on choice. She was simply doing her job; imperfectly, maybe, but earnestly.

Stoicism teaches compassion before judgment, understanding before outrage. That night, I failed to live up to that ideal. I let my emotions drive my reaction. I drifted from the person I wanted to be; I was not the person Ellie needed me to be. I knew I had to make it right.

The next day, I apologized. Not just because it was polite, but because it was necessary - the first step in realignment. If I was going to lead my family through this, I couldn't afford to lose myself in the process. If we were going to endure, it had to start with how we treated the people walking alongside us, even when we were at our worst.

The realization stayed with me long after the apology. Something in me began to change. It wasn't all at once, but subtly, almost imperceptibly. My focus shifted away from control and toward steadiness. From fixing and planning everything to simply being present for what was.

I felt my role begin to transform. I wasn't just a father or husband or friend anymore. I was becoming something else entirely: a support beam, a buffer, a calm in a world that no longer offered predictability or order. This wasn't a strategic, conscious decision, but a quiet adaption to necessity. Ellie didn't need a version of me who panicked every time her numbers dropped or spiraled with each medical term. She needed someone who could absorb the chaos without reflecting it back. Someone steady enough to make the unbearable feel survivable, if only for a moment.

At first, I tried to create the steadiness by controlling everything around me, like the schedules, the medications, or the side effects. I thought if I could just understand enough, plan enough, prepare enough, I could somehow bend reality back into shape. And to an extent, that was true. Preparation has its place. But ultimate control over the external world is an illusion. The more I reached outward, the more it slipped away. What I really needed to master wasn't my environment or the expanding glossary of medical terms. It was my own mind.

If we were going to survive years of treatment, it would demand as much mental resilience as physical strength. I needed to become an observer, a learner, a steady and stable force.

"You have power over your mind - not outside events," Aurelius wrote. "Realize this, and you will find strength." (*Meditations,* 6.8)

That became my goal. Not control. Not certainty. Strength.

Ellie, Emily, and even the rest of our family needed to see something steady in me. Sometimes that meant speaking with quiet optimism even when I didn't feel it. Other times it meant hugging family members and assuring them we trusted the plan. And sometimes, it just meant being able to laugh.

Laughter, I was learning, could be its own kind of medicine.

As part of Ellie's post-surgery care, doctors prescribed a low-dose steroid to help her body recover from the toll of the drugs. They warned it could make her emotional, moody, and volatile. We didn't fully appreciate what that meant until a few days later.

One afternoon, Ellie refused to eat anything from the hospital. Her appetite had already been inconsistent, but she badly needed nutrients to build strength. I took a deep breath and crouched beside her bed, trying my best to summon the calm, measured father I wanted to be.

"Ellie," I said gently, "Mommy and Daddy really want to make sure you get some food in your belly. What sounds good to you? What can I get?"

Without missing a beat, Ellie locked eyes with me, stone faced and serious, and let out a roar so primal, so ferocious, it shook the room.

"I. WANT. OLIVES."

I'm pretty sure the entire pediatric floor heard her scream.

If you've never had a steroid-fueled toddler scream "olives" in your face like a Roman emperor ordering a siege, you haven't lived. For five seconds, I was genuinely afraid. She held eye contact like a disapproving boss ready to revoke my parenting license if I didn't bring those olives, pronto.

Weeks ago, this would've been a serious parenting moment. I might've sat Ellie down and tried to explain respect or tone, maybe set a boundary about speaking politely. But I was sleep deprived, emotionally wrecked, and living off hospital coffee.

So instead, I just laughed.

I laughed because it was the only sane thing to do in that moment. Because it reminded me that we were still human, still here. Because Ellie, the tiny warrior hooked up to wires and medications, demanded olives like a tyrant on a rampage.

Then, something amazing happened.

Ellie laughed too.

"Daddy, you're funny," she giggled.

"Me?" I replied, "you're the one screaming about olives!"

"I *do* want olives!" she screamed again, this time with a grin.

And just like that, in a hospital room filled with uncertainty, we found a moment to laugh. It wasn't planned or poetic. It was ridiculous, loud, and perfect.

I had spent years philosophizing about mental strength, stoicism, and mindfulness. That day, I learned that all that wisdom sometimes looks less like meditations or mantras, and more like a jar of medium-sized, pitted black olives.

6

A Temporary Home

Each of the thirty days of Induction brought new challenges and small victories. There were fears, yes, but also triumphs. We had been plunged into darkness with no end in sight. But slowly, day by day, we began to see glimmers of light, distant but real. We learned to celebrate them.

When she was first admitted, Ellie's initial lack of energy was due in large part to severe anemia. Her blood couldn't carry enough oxygen from her lungs to the rest of her body. The measure for this is hemoglobin, a protein found in red blood cells. For a normal three year old child, hemoglobin levels should be between 11.5 and 13.5 g/dL. Anything below 7 is considered critical.

On the day of her diagnosis, Ellie's level was 3.

Medically, it was life-threatening. She was at risk of organ damage, even organ failure. One nurse told us that she couldn't believe Ellie had been able to stand when we brought her in.

But within a week, we saw a transformation. Ellie responded well to her first blood transfusions and medications. Her white blood cell count, once over 80,000, dropped to just 400. Each day, we saw more of her returned to us. Where there had once been only darkness, we found glimpses of the daughter we knew, a little stronger than the day before.

On Day 8, Ellie slept through the night. The next morning, she felt strong enough to take a walk around the oncology floor. It was the first time we had seen her up and walking around since we arrived. As we passed the nurses station, one of them pulled me aside.

"We talk about Ellie every day," she said. "I've been working with children for twenty years and your daughter is the smartest and kindest three year old I've ever met. Her vocabulary is better than most five year olds. She is going to beat this disease. You know that, right?"

I had been telling myself that very thing each night: Ellie will beat this. Life will return to normal soon. But even as I whispered it to myself in the dark, I didn't know if I fully believed it. I was terrified of what news might come the next morning.

Every night, I fell asleep replaying that first call from Emily, the cold of the hotel room, the bass thumping from the music next door. I'd try to will myself into confidence, but the fear never subsided. I was always waiting for that next phone call or the next test result. For something else to fall apart.

But the nurse's words hit different. There was no performance in her voice, no obligation in her tone. She wasn't saying what people were supposed to say. She was meant it, deeply and completely.

For the first time, I believed it. I believed we'd be okay.

That belief grew stronger with each day Ellie conquered. The way she laughed at her favorite movies. The joy on her face as she played in the oncology's unit's playroom. The first time we sat together and ate dinner at a normal hour in her hospital room. These small wins added up. For a time, life felt almost normal again.

But around every corner, reminders waited. They were always there, quiet but ready to strike.

One morning, during a routine walk around the floor, Ellie tripped and bumper her head on the linoleum. For most toddlers, this would have been a quick hug and kiss, then back to playing. But Ellie wasn't most toddlers. Not now.

Her blood had virtually no platelets left.

Platelets are the body's first responders. They are cell fragments that race toward injuries to form clots and stop bleeding. Without them, blood can't clot. Ellie had no responders, no natural defense.

Within minutes, a large, swollen lump formed on her forehead, dark and translucent. We could see the blood pooling, trapped with nowhere to go.

The doctors moved quickly. In cases like this, they justifiably assume the worst. Ellie was rushed to CT scans and given an immediate platelet infusion. Nurses stayed in our room for hours afterward, watching for signs of concussion or internal bleeding.

A hospital bracelet labeled 'Fall Risk' was secured to her wrist. From that moment on, she wasn't allowed to get out of bed unless escorted by staff.

The fall was a jarring reminder of how precarious Ellie's situation was. It had been easy to grow complacent: to see color in her cheeks again, to hear her giggle, to believe that maybe the worst part of this battle was behind us.

It wasn't. Not even close.

The swelling on Ellie's head faded after a few days. She avoided any serious injury. But our fears lingered.

Weeks earlier, we'd been jolted awake by the fragility of life. Now that awareness lived with us, woven into each hour of the day. We remained on high alert, not because we wanted to, but because we had no other choice.

The fall had also reminded us how fortunate we truly were.

Up until now, we had seen ourselves as victims of randomness. We were cruelly dealt a bad hand for no reason at all. I'd long since stopped asking *why* this happened, stopped searching for meaning or cosmic fairness. We were unlucky, plain and simple. Trapped in a nightmare that no one chose.

But the slow, quiet mornings walking the oncology floor began to put that view into sharper focus. So did the fact that Ellie's fall, terrifying as it was, hadn't ended in something worse.

Yes, she had cancer. Yes, she would endure years of grueling treatments, pain, and fear. But in that hospital, we saw what the other end of misfortunate looked like. We saw what it meant when hope was no longer part of the plan.

We saw children who had been there for months, some for years. Children with more aggressive diagnoses, lower odds, and parents who spoke in hushed tones with doctors just outside their doors. We saw parents who had stopped trying to count the days.

Ellie was sick, but she was getting better. That was more than many other parents could say.

We had a diagnosis. A treatment plan. Doctors who were skilled, confident, and deeply invested in our daughter's care. We had a village behind us, holding us up. We had reason to believe that our story, however long and painful, might one day return to something resembling normal life.

For the first time since this journey began, I didn't feel cursed. I felt something else, something quieter, creep in. It wasn't some divine intervention or silver lining, but the recognition our luck. The understanding that randomness has no limits to its cruelty, yet we had been spared the worst.

Rather than framing our situation in terms of misfortune, I could choose to see what *wasn't*. To recognize the alternate realities we'd narrowly escaped.

Most importantly, it was an acknowledgement of what we still had. It was the thing that had been ripped away from so many of the families around us: we had hope.

That hope was built on a foundation of celebrating every win, no matter how small, and doing so together. Throughout Ellie's treatment, we kept a group chat we called "Ellie's Family." It became a running journal of small victories and moments of grace we shared with immediate and extended family. Each day, we'd send updates with the latest Ellie news. Sometimes there was big news to share: test results, milestones, or side effects she managed to avoid.

Most often, though, our updates were snapshots of the tiny, ordinary moments we had learned to deliberately celebrate. A funny comment Ellie made. The nap she finally took. The time she insisted on eating pasta and meatballs for breakfast. The group chat became a kind of shared journey, a living narrative that allowed us to shape the story we were living through and define it on our own terms.

We made a conscious decision to highlight the positives. To count our fortunes rather than misfortunes. To frame the chaos with humor whenever we could, because sometimes laughter was the only power we had left. This wasn't denial or naive optimism; it was a willful effort carry on with our heads held high.

After one sleepless night, a nurse came in to record what Ellie had eaten the day before. I had just woken up and was still rubbing the sleep from eyes when he entered the room.

"Ellie's vitals look good today," he started, "what about food or drinks?"

"No food, all good here, thank you." I mumbled.

He paused, pen in hand, and looked up at me. "No food?"

"Yeah, I'm not hungry yet." I said, still half asleep.

There was a beat of silence. Then, deadpan: "Sir, I'm asking what *your daughter* ate yesterday. I'm not here to take *your* order."

Naturally, this exchange made its way into the group chat and I was teased about it for weeks. That morning could've been remembered as just another sleep-deprived, emotionally draining day. Instead, it became one of our favorite stories. A funny moment we chose to hold on to.

We were learning to choose our memories. We didn't pretend everything was okay; we chose which moments were worth keeping.

71

Framing, I had learned, was every bit as important as framework. It was only chaos if we framed it that way. These events - the diagnosis, the fall, the long battle ahead - were not happening *to* us. They were simply happening. We might not have had control over the external forces at play, but we did have control over how we approached them, how we framed them, and what we chose to carry forward.

Thanksgiving Day was the first real test of that mindset. It was the first major holiday since the diagnosis and we would be spending it away from all friends and family.

My incredible aunt surprised us with a full Thanksgiving meal delivered right to the hospital, complete with a box full of pastries, donuts, and pie for dessert. It was a gracious act of love, a reminder that we were still surrounded by people who cared, even if they couldn't be in the room with us.

Ellie, still navigating steroids and a rocky appetite, latched onto one thing immediately: that pumpkin pie. She ate a slice after every meal for a week. To this day, she still talks about that pie (the marshmallow topping, especially) as the best dessert she's ever had.

Thanksgiving weekend gave more to be thankful for: we learned that we were on track to complete Induction by the first week of December. Ellie's third birthday was on December 6th, and doctors believed we just might be home in time to blow out birthday candles.

The thought of Ellie unwrapping birthday presents, smiling as we sang "Happy Birthday" felt surreal. It was more than a dream: it was a plan. Our optimism and mental framing weren't just coping strategies anymore; they were beginning to reflect reality. We craved that kind of normal, and now, it finally felt within reach.

Thanksgiving was also a reminder of how much we missed Rosie.

It was easy to forget, in that chaos of chemo schedules and medication protocols, that she was enduring her own quiet battle. Nearly three weeks had passed since she had been at home with us. Three weeks wondering why her Mommy and Daddy weren't there to wake her up each morning or read her a bedtime story each night. We video called and exchanged daily updates from our parents, but nothing could replace the feeling of her tiny arms wrapping around us in a hug.

She had no idea where we were or what was happening to Ellie, and wouldn't for quite some time. We missed her more than words could explain.

That Thanksgiving weekend, I decided to see Rosie in person now that Ellie's health was improving. I'd bring her some lunch, play with her for a few hours, then head back to the hospital. Ellie's doctors were comfortable with this plan so long as Rosie showed no signs of illness. With Ellie's immune system nearly nonexistent, even a mild cold could become dangerous. Rosie seemed perfectly healthy. We had her take a COVID test out of an abundance of caution. It came back negative. We were in the clear.

I'd finally get to hold her again.

On the day of my visit, I stood waiting for the elevator just outside of the Pediatric Oncology Unit. A family nearby huddled together, visibly shaken. A woman my age was sobbing into her hands, her partner's arm wrapped tightly around her. The elevator dinged. An older couple walked out and approached the family in the lobby.

Just before the elevator doors closed, I heard the words: "She's in a better place now."

A lump rose in my throat. My eyes filled before I even reached the ground floor. When the doors opened, I could still hear their cries echoing from three stories up.

It was a sobering reminder of the fragility of everything. Of the truths we couldn't outrun. For all our progress and precision of modern medicine, tragedy hovered just beyond our rainbow-colored door. We thought we had heard the worst words a parent could hear.

But we hadn't.

That family had.

And in that moment, I realized again: we were the lucky ones. Ellie would get to leave this place. I'd replay that elevator encounter countless times over the years: not as source of paralyzing fear, but as a willful, humbling wake-up call.

Like the Stoics before me, I found that reflecting on the tragedies that could have been, and those that might yet come, grounded me in the present. No smile is sweeter, no giggle more joyful, than when you know just how fragile those moments really are. There will *always* be someone who has it worse, always someone would trade places with me in a heartbeat. Even here, living out of a duffle bag and surviving on hospital cafeteria bagels, there was so much to be grateful for.

I sat in my car and wiped tears from my eyes. *Positive framing*, I reminded myself. I was about to see Rosie. That mattered most in this moment.

When I walked through the door of Emily's parents house, Rosie crawled so fast toward me that she lost her balance and toppled over. She popped back up, wobbled, and flung herself into my arms.

I scooped her up and got the warmest, tightest hug I'd had in weeks. I'm still not sure who needed it more.

Rosie and I played for hours. We built towering block castles, played hide and seek, and read books together under a blanket on the living room floor. She never once left my side.

I FaceTimed Ellie, too. By any measure, it was the happiest I'd seen her since she was admitted. From the moment Rosie was born, Ellie had been the best big sister. She was protective, patient, and completely devoted. The two were inseparable. Every morning, Ellie would wake up and ask over and over when it was time to get her little sister.

They hadn't seen each other in weeks. I didn't fully grasp just how much they missed each other until their laughter echoed through my phone's tiny speaker. In that moment, it was so clear: they needed each other just as much as they needed us.

As I said my goodbye's to Rosie, it struck me that I wouldn't see her again until our trip back to North Carolina. I pictured her laughter in the same room as Ellie's instead of through a phone camera. I imagined them waking up in their new bedrooms, running down the hall for their good morning hug like nothing had ever pulled them apart.

The past three weeks had felt like an eternity of fear and separation. But the next few weeks promised to be different. There would still be hospital visits and precautions, but there would also be the simple joy of our girls together under one roof again. We would build moments of light strong enough to outweigh the darkness.

7

Isolation, Reunion

I drove back to the hospital that evening feeling more whole than I had in weeks. I fell asleep in the recliner next to Ellie's bed, picturing the four of us together in our new home. I could almost hear the laughter and feel the hugs. More than anything, I craved normalcy.

The next morning, that vision slipped through my fingers.

A single phone call: Rosie had been exposed to COVID. Emily's parents tested positive, too. I had spent nearly the entire afternoon with them just a day ago. There hadn't been a single warning sign: no coughs, no fevers, no reason to suspect anything was wrong. Life had felt normal for the first time in weeks, and then, in a span of thirty seconds, that illusion shattered. The ground shifted again, without notice, without mercy.

The realization hit like a punch to the chest: if there was any chance I was sick, I couldn't be anywhere near Ellie or Emily. Ellie's immune system was still virtually nonexistent;

a mild cold could wreck havoc. COVID could be catastrophic.

There was no time to think, only to act. I slipped on an N95 mask over my face, threw clothes and toiletries into my duffle bag, and walked out of the hospital room. Less than ten minutes after the call, I was already in my car in the hospital parking garage.

I slammed my fists against the steeling wheel in frustration. Just a day ago, I had felt the warmth of normal life returning. I had daydreamed about the promise of home and our family together under one roof again. Now, that fragile hope had been ripped away overnight.

The old feelings of fear, guilt, and helplessness I had when Ellie was diagnosed came rushing back in an instant. What if Ellie tested positive? How long will it be until I see her again? What if Emily got sick, too? Would she have to leave Ellie alone in that hospital room?

I sat in the car for what felt like forever, trying to catch my breath. For a moment, I was swallowed by the randomness, the sheer unfairness of it all. One chromosome error, one virus, one slip, and the fragile scaffolding of our life teetered again.

Then I thought back to the same Marcus Aurelius line I'd repeated to myself so many times: *You have power over your mind, not outside events.* It was the same lesson that had carried me through the diagnosis, the same reminder I'd clung to when I snapped at the nurse, when I held Ellie through her rage, when I watched the elevator doors close on someone else's tragedy. There was only one thing I was in control over: my own mind.

I needed to act, not dwell on what I couldn't change. We no longer had a home in New Jersey. Driving eight hours to North Carolina now felt impossible. I just needed somewhere to wait.

Instead of heading south right away, I drove to my parents' house. It felt like the safest middle ground: close enough if I was needed, but far enough to protect Ellie. They had an extra bedroom tucked away from the rest of the house. I'd lock myself in there for the next 48 hours. If I tested positive for COVID, I'd leave immediately for North Carolina.

That night, sleep never came. I lay awake for hours, my mind spinning with what-ifs. What if I'd unknowingly brought the virus into Ellie's hospital room? What if I drove to North Carolina, only to find out Ellie's condition worsened?

At 3 a.m., I grabbed the thermometer on the night stand. 101.4° F.

I stared at the number, a dull numbness settling in. Another twist of randomness. Another test of endurance. I closed my eyes and reminded myself, as I had so many times before. *This is happening - now what?*

I took a COVID test and it confirmed what I had already knew: positive. The faint, double line on the stick was strangely comforting. It gave me clarity, however unwelcome. It was proof that leaving the hospital was the right decision. It also freed me to move past the unknown and toward whatever came next.

For the first time, I felt almost empowered by the bad news. I couldn't change the virus, but I could control what I did next.

Though I had stayed overnight at the hospital after my visit to Rosie, the timing made it unlikely that I would have been contagious then. Thankfully, Emily called later that morning with the kind of good news we'd learned not to take for granted: she and Ellie had both tested negative.

With that confirmation, the next step was clear: get to North Carolina.

In my mind, I could see two ways to frame the situation. I could, understandably, sulk in the unfairness of it all. What was supposed to be our big move together became just me and a single duffle bag, driving to an empty house that wouldn't feel like home yet. For the second time in a month, I'd be hundreds of miles away from my cancer-stricken daughter.

All of that was true, but for the first time, I felt no need to give it space in my mind. Thoughts of guilt and resentment wouldn't change anything. They wouldn't move me one step closer to what mattered most: being ready when my family could join me.

So I chose the second framing. Emily, Ellie, and Rosie would arrive in North Carolina in about ten days. By then, I'd hopefully be COVID-free. That gave me ten days to unpack, make the house feel warm and welcome, and transform four walls and a roof into something that could carry the promise we'd all been clinging to.

When I opened that front door for the first time, it wouldn't feel like home yet. But by the time they walked through it, it could. That was all the motivation I needed to put the next foot forward.

The two main routes from New Jersey to North Carolina are Interstate 95 or Interstate 81. I-95 hugs the East Coast, threading through the congestion of Philadelphia, Baltimore, and Washington D.C. It's the route every map app recommends, shaving off fifty miles on paper, but rarely saves time in reality. I'd driven it plenty of times before, but it never felt right for this journey.

Instead, I chose the longer way down. I-81 cuts through Pennsylvania's hills and dips south through the rolling farmland of Virginia before it finally slips into North Carolina. It's a route I've always loved for its quiet beauty. Winding roads lead into a steady procession of mountains and valleys, each ridge fading into the next like brushstrokes in layered shades of blue.

There's one stretch near the Virginia-North Carolina state line that never fails to leave me awestruck: the Fancy Gap. Just past the *Welcome to North Carolina* sign, the road hooks into a wide, sweeping curve and drops into a steep downgrade. On a clear day, the view is breathtaking. The sky doubles in size, opening to reveal the ridges of the Piedmont rolling toward the horizon and the jagged crowns of the Blue Ridge Mountains in the distance.

This time, the view hit differently. In another life, I'd imagined Emily, Ellie, Rosie, and me together in the car, all of us cheering as we crossed the state line. It would be the first real sign that our new beginning was just waiting beyond the mountain. But that dream, like so many lately, had to bend to reality.

So I watched the ridges appear and recede, the horizon rolling toward me as I drove. The mountains ahead were beautiful, but they were also obstacles I'd have to cross alone before I could call this place home for all of us.

I pulled into our new driveway just as the sun slipped below the North Carolina treetops. The movers had already dropped off the boxes and furniture we'd packed up what felt like a lifetime ago. I sat there for a moment, alone in the car, staring at the front door. I imaged the sea of bubble wrap, cardboard, and cold medication that waited me on the other side.

Yet again, I had a choice. Still nursing a low grade fever and the body aches that come with COVID, I could walk into that home and exist in quiet isolation for a week. I could make due with the bare essentials, leaving the heavy lifting for when Emily came down to help. I could spend the days moping about my luck and the unfairness of it all. I could set my duffel bag on the bare hardwood floor and let the silence swallow me whole.

But what would it look like to make the most of this moment?

I sat up straighter. There were over 80 boxes to unpack, less than ten a day if I paced myself right. I'd need to hang TVs on the walls, swap smoke detector batteries, and assemble the furniture. New appliances were set to arrive later in the week, too. We had a cleaner scheduled to do a deep disinfecting in two days. Maybe I'd push that to the day before Emily and the girls arrived, so they'd walk into a fresh, welcoming space.

I started scribbling down the tasks. For the first time in days, that growing to do list felt like a purpose, like something fully in my control. This was how I could make the most of this moment: not just surviving here alone, but shaping this empty house into something ready for my family's return. I would hold this space for them and protect the hope we all needed.

I felt a spark of defiance flare up in my chest, a chip on my shoulder against the chaos of the past month. This wasn't how I imagined arriving at our new house. But pity wouldn't build a home for my girls. Action would.

When I finally opened the door and stepped onto the driveway, the North Carolina air was noticeably warmer than what I had left behind in New Jersey. I took a deep breath, walked up the steps, and FaceTimed Emily. I needed us to walk through through that front door together whether or not she was physically here.

The door swung open to a vast emptiness. Every footstep echoed. Walls were bare. Cardboard boxes were stacked like makeshift barricades in every room, each one labeled in thick black marker: *Kitchen, Toys, Ellie's Room.*

I dropped my bag by the door and wandered from room to room, phone camera in hand, showing Emily every corner. This house had been an idea for so long. It was a promise, a fresh start, a better place for the girls to build new memories. It looked hollow now, like an unfinished sentence waiting for the words that would bring it to life. But soon, Ellie and Rosie would walk through this front door, and we'd have our whole lives ahead of us. Cancer wouldn't take that away.

When the call with Emily ended, the silence pressed in around me, but I let it be just that. Silence. Not loneliness, not despair. Just the quiet hum of a house waiting to become a home.

I grabbed the nearest boxes, tore through the packing tape, and immediately started to work. I made a game of it, challenging myself to keep moving through the boxes at record pace. I ate a takeout dinner standing up, installing new locks on the doors and stacking plates in kitchen cabinets in between forkfuls.

Every stuffed animal, every children's book, and every tiny pair of shoes all reminded me of who I was doing this for. I paused to catch my breath only to pump hand sanitizer or down another cough drop. It was nearly midnight.

I wasn't done yet.

I turned to the kitchen and eyed the flat-packed boxes that held our new dining set. One day soon, we'd share pancakes around that table and blow out birthday candles for the girls. We'd host new friends for dinner and play board games late into the night. Every room in this house held a vision of what life could be like; every box was a chance to bring that vision closer.

Two hours later, the table stood finished. Eight chairs surrounded it, waiting to hold the people I loved most.

Exhausted, I stumbled into the playroom. It was the one place that already looked like Ellie and Rosie had been here. Their books, toys, and stuffed animals were carefully placed around the room. It reminded me what I was working toward. I laid down on the undersized yellow loveseat, the only piece of furniture ready for sleep. There were no beds ready for me, no linens to lay out. Just that small sofa under the glow of a single lamp. I don't even remember closing my eyes.

My phone alarm rang just a few hours later. I forced myself upright, my body stiff and my head hazy from the lingering virus. Within minutes, I had found the coffee maker buried in one of the kitchen boxes and fired it up, pouring the first cup into an old travel mug I'd dug out the night before.

Time to get back to work.

I moved from room to room like a man on a mission. Each box I broke down made the space feel less like a warehouse and more like a home. By the third day, the cardboard towers were gone, flattened and stacked neatly by the curb for recycling. Every stuffed animal found a shelf. Every dish found a cabinet. The girls' books lined their tiny white bookcases, waiting for bedtime stories that were still yet to come.

This wasn't the homecoming I had pictured, but in the quiet, steady work of these days, I was the building the foundation for the one we deserved. There was something meditative in it. Each task, no matter how small, was a way of reclaiming control from the chaos that had defined our lives. I couldn't change the randomness of a chromosome mutation or the bad luck of a virus, but I could decide how this home would feel when they walked through the door.

On the afternoon of December 2nd, that homecoming took a gigantic leap toward becoming a reality. 31 days after we first brought Ellie to the hospital, she was officially cleared for discharge. Induction was finally over. For the first time in over a month, she would get to feel sunlight on her face and taste a warm, home-cooked meal.

But she wouldn't be coming home to North Carolina just yet. I was still positive and contagious with COVID, so that walk through our new front door would have to wait.

That night, Emily drove Ellie to my parents' house, not far from the hospital. She sent the sweetest photo of Ellie fast asleep, a stuffed animal tucked under each arm. There would be no interruptions for vitals, no IV medication changes, no beeps from the heart rate monitor.

For a moment, all seemed normal. Anyone that saw that photo would not have guessed she'd spent the past month in a hospital bed or endured hours of chemotherapy. In that picture, she was just a kid, holding her favorite stuffed animal, dreaming of whatever made her happiest.

I went to bed that night at 3 a.m., eyes glazed over from reading furniture assembly instructions by the dim glow of my phone. When my head finally hit the pillow, I felt the calmest I had in weeks. Knowing Ellie was safe, home, and comfortable was the sigh of relief I had been so desperate for. We still had two years of this journey ahead, but for now, I was learning to celebrate the milestones along the way.

December 4th, my birthday, arrived without fanfare. I turned 33 alone, hundreds of miles from my loved ones, but it didn't bother me much. The day wasn't about me; it was just another day to build furniture, install security cameras, and fix toilets. I was on a mission.

That resolve only strengthened when Ellie FaceTimed to wish me a Happy Birthday. I took her on another virtual tour of the house, this time showing her the bedroom she'd soon sleep in. Her face lit up when she saw her toys and stuffed animals she had packed over a month ago.

Before Ellie was born, we thought she might share a birthday with me. December 4th came and doctors told us she would likely arrive that night. But she had other plans. She waited nearly two more days, until December 6th, to join our world.

When she wished me a Happy Birthday that night, she reminded me that hers was coming up soon

"Daddy! Do you know I'm going to be three?" she beamed, her head nodding in excitement.

"I sure do!" I laughed. "You're going to get the biggest birthday cake ever this year."

"Are you going to come here and have some with us?" she asked, still not quite understanding why I wasn't there to welcome her home.

"Oh Ellie," I said, wishing I could hug her through the screen. "You know I want that more than anything in the world. But soon, you're going to come here to your new home. I promise I'll save the biggest slice of cake just for you."

She pressed her lips against the camera, pretending to kiss me goodnight. In that moment, I wasn't thinking about how unfair it felt to be so far away. The distance didn't feel like a punishment. Separation wasn't on my mind.

When I turned off the lights that night and crawled into my makeshift bed, I didn't lie awake haunted by what cancer or COVID had taken away. I fell asleep thinking only of what we were about to get back.

On the morning of Ellie's birthday, I FaceTimed her to wish her a Happy Birthday. By the time I called, she had already devoured a slice of cake.

"Daddy, guess what?" she said, her eyes wide, brimming with mischief.

"What is it, Ellie?" I replied.

"Three years ago, I came out of Mommy's belly," she declared with total confidence.

"Oh really?" I stammered, unsure how to follow up a statement like that coming from a toddler.

86

"Yep," she nodded. "I asked Mommy to go back in her belly today, but she said no. Can you ask her again for me?"

It was probably the hardest I'd laughed since the day Ellie was diagnosed. Day by day, hour by hour, we were getting our Ellie back: the silly, sharp little girl who could always surprise us. A single chromosome error had taken her spark away for a while, but we were clawing it back in waves. I could hear it in every phone call, see it in every grin.

On December 9th, free from COVID, I finally got to see that smile in person. Emily, Ellie, and Rosie drove down to North Carolina to our new home and we were finally together again.

I remember pacing our front hallway that afternoon, glancing through the front door every few minutes as if that might make their car appear faster. I was so eager to start our life together, so anxious to have the page turned on this next chapter.

When I finally saw their car pull into our driveway, a weight I'd been carrying for over a month seemed to melt right there on the hardwood floor. I threw open the car door before they could turn off the engine. Ellie's smile beamed at me through the window, brighter and sweeter than I'd remembered.

Emily stepped out first, then Rosie, sleepy but curious about this new place. And then Ellie, brave and fragile and so unmistakably her, hopped down from the car and ran straight into my arms.

After 31 days of hospital walls, of masked hugs and cautious goodnights, we were finally together again. We stepped through the front door, side by side, as a family. The future was ours to reclaim.

For a few moments, I let myself believe that the worst was behind us. Maybe we'd paid our share of life's cruelty and come out of the other side. The next two years wouldn't be easy, we knew that much. But I told myself that at least we'd face it under one roof, no more living out of duffle bags or drifting to sleep to the sound of heart monitors.

The truth is, the two years that followed would test our family in ways I couldn't yet imagine. The battles ahead would push us to the edge of ourselves, time and time again. Whatever framework I thought I mastered, whatever steadiness I thought I'd found, would soon be brought to its breaking point.

But we had already proved what happens when you keep moving forward, when you keep putting one foot in front of the other. Whatever darkness waited for us, whatever storms were gathering just beyond this point, we'd face them together.

We thought we had already discovered the limits of what we could endure. The next two years would stretch those limits farther than we ever thought possible.

8
North Carolina

We had barely finished unpacking before we dragged the Christmas decorations out of the garage. Ellie lit up when she saw the strands of twinkling lights and the giant plastic tub filled with ornaments and stockings. Rosie trailed behind her, giggling as she grabbed hold of a plush snowman she would keep by her side for months to come.

There was something beautifully ordinary about it. The four of us were in our new living room, building our own 'normal' in spite of everything. Outside, the North Carolina sun was still warm enough to make you forget it was December. But inside, we were dancing to Jingle Bells and writing letters to Santa, letting ourselves believe for a few hours that we could press pause on the chaos.

It was our first Christmas in this house and the first time we felt like we'd reclaimed a little piece of life for ourselves. We didn't have to think about hospital visits or lab results, only about untangling the stubborn knots of string lights and watching our girls laugh as they tore tissue paper from gift bags.

Things felt normal, at least for these first few weeks. 'Normal' had changed its meaning, but we clung to it anyway, knowing how easily it could be taken from us again.

After the move, Ellie's treatment shifted to a hospital and clinic in Charlotte, about thirty minutes from our new home. While I worked, Emily spent hours in waiting rooms and treatment chairs, bringing Ellie to chemotherapy appointments two, sometimes three times a week.

We were settling into our new routines of treatment days, work calls, and nap times that never seemed to line up. We held it together, but not without the help we were lucky enough to have along the way.

Shortly after we moved, my sister and parents followed us down to North Carolina. They uprooted their lives for many of the same reasons we did. My sister and her husband were just starting a family, excited for the promise of new experiences together. My parents, in true European fashion, never wanted to be more than a few miles away from their kids. Both my parents and my sister moved a block away from our new home.

Their support along Ellie's journey is something I will be eternally grateful for. Every diaper change, every warm meal brought over after a long day at the clinic, every evening spent watching Rosie so Emily and I could rest or take Ellie to the hospital: it all mattered. It all made a difference. It was a critical reason why were able to keep going.

It was the quiet, ordinary help that kept our fragile sense of normal from tipping over completely. Rosie could play with her cousin, Luca, while Ellie recovered from another round of chemo. Emily and I could take difficult calls with doctors while my mom snuck in to put dinner on the table for the girls.

Emily's family helped too, even from afar. Back in New Jersey, they never missed a single day of FaceTime calls with the girls. They visited often, and never once forgot to bring down real New Jersey bagels that we just couldn't find in North Carolina. Their visits became little lifelines, like bursts of familiarity that reminded us of home before everything changed.

Sometimes they'd show up with trunkfuls of food, toys for the girls, and a kind of energy that made the house feel lighter for a few days. Ellie would light up at the sound of her grandparents' voices, or spend the entire weekend playing games with her aunts and uncles.

When they couldn't be here in person, they were still part of our daily rhythm. Even through a screen, they managed to make us feel surrounded by love. The distance never stopped them from showing up in every way that mattered.

Looking back, there's no way we could have survived those early months without the support of family and friends. They were the safety net when everything else felt like it could unravel at any moment.

Fighting cancer wasn't something we could, or had to, do alone. It took a village. We were lucky enough to have one.

For a while, that village helped us hold onto a version of normal. For the first few weeks, it almost looked like life had settled into something predictable. But we were never more than one fever, one stray virus, one lab result away from being reminded just how fragile that normal really was.

It didn't take long. Just six weeks into this new life, we found ourselves right back where we thought we had left behind: back in an emergency room, sitting under the bright fluorescent lights, holding Ellie's tiny hand while we waited to see what would come next.

It started on an ordinary weeknight after dinner. Ellie barely touched her plate. It was another side effect of chemo we were learning to accept. She wandered over to the couch, too drained even for our nightly dance parties.

Emily pressed her hand to Ellie's forehead and looked at me with eyes that said it all. We didn't have to speak. We knew.

The thermometer confirmed what we feared: Ellie had spiked a fever. Leukemia protocol is painfully clear: any fever means an immediate trip to the emergency room. With no immune system to fight a virus or infection, her tiny body couldn't do it alone.

We knew nights like this would come, but knowing didn't make it feel any less terrifying. My mind swirled through what-ifs and worst case scenarios. Until now, Ellie had one battle to fight: leukemia. As Emily packed a bag for the hospital room, I realized that there were hundreds more battles ahead. Tonight was only the first of many.

Every sneeze, every warm forehead, every close encounter with a stranger who might be sick - they were all reminders of the invisible threats surrounding us. The reality of the next two years hit me like a freight train. *This* was our new normal.

We decided that Emily would take Ellie to the hospital and I would stay at home with Rosie, hoping they'd be back before sunrise.

They weren't.

By morning, we learned Ellie caught some sort of virus. A healthy toddler might have shrugged it off without a second thought, but Ellie needed round-the-clock monitoring to make sure the infection didn't spiral into something worse. The doctors told us that she would likely need to stay another day, maybe two. She'd have to be fever-free and might need another blood transfusion before she could come home.

The next day, my sister was able to watch Rosie as I went to the hospital to be with Emily and Ellie. The drive to the hospital was silent. My mind wandered down every dark corridor, rehearsing every worst-case scenario I couldn't control.

Then I caught myself spiraling. I thought back to the mental framework I'd leaned on since that first diagnosis day: *This happened. Now what?* It wasn't a cure for fear, but it gave the fear somewhere to sit. It was my anchor when the swirl of unknowns threatened to pull me under.

Ellie has a fever. Now what?

Now we wait. Now we listen to the doctors, the experts. Now we remind ourselves that there's a plan in place for situations like this.

That mindset didn't break her fever or make the hospital walls feel any less suffocating. But it made the moment feel like something we could stand inside of, instead of being swallowed by it. We couldn't control the virus, the transfusions, or the endless lab results. But we could control our footing, our response. That had to be enough.

When I walked into Ellie's hospital room, she was sitting upright in bed, a coloring book spread across her lap. Her

93

cheeks were puffed from IV fluids, her skin still pale from the fever that wouldn't quite let go. But her eyes lit up the moment she saw me.

"Daddy!" she squealed, throwing her arms wide.

"Ellie!" I laughed, matching her tone. "How's my big girl feeling today?"

She grinned and puffed up her chest, ready to brag. "Good! I stayed up so, so late last night. Mommy let me have chips for a snack even though it was bedtime!" She shook her head in disbelief, like she had pulled off the greatest heist in history. "I'm coloring now but Mommy said I can watch TV later."

I sat down on the edge of her bed, careful not to disturb the tangle of IV lines snaking around the port in her chest. She held up her crayon masterpiece with a proud little smirk, waiting for my reaction.

"It's beautiful Ellie, I love it," I told her. And I did. But what really caught me was the way she beamed at something so simple, so ordinary, in a place that was anything but.

There was something both devastating and awe-inspiring about it. This hospital room should have weighed her down. The beeping monitors, the chemical smell, the hush of nurses' shoes in the hallway: it should have scared her. It terrified me.

But to Ellie, it was just another place to color. Just another story she will tell her friends and family about how she got to stay up late and eat chips in bed.

At three years old, she didn't know enough to dread what might come next. She didn't understand the gravity of the situation she was in or how sick she really was. She didn't lie awake wondering how her body would handle the next round of chemo, or whether the fever would creep back in. She didn't bargain with the universe or question why this was happening to her.

I'd spent years studying frameworks for acceptance. I read the Stoics, filling the margins of Seneca and Marcus Aurelius with underlines and notes to self. I memorized lines from Plato and Socrates about the nature of the good life. I practiced breathing exercises and meditation. I taught myself to focus on the moment, to squeeze every drop from it, to accept what is, to always ask: *Now what?*

And yet here was my daughter, barefoot in a hospital gown, living that truth by instinct alone.

It broke me and put me back together in the same breath.

Ellie reminded me that sometimes the greatest strength is the kind that doesn't think itself strong at all. It just keeps coloring, chip crumbs on the bedsheets, IV line taped to her chest, laughing at a cartoon while the world keeps spinning.

She didn't need philosophy to tell her what to do with pain. She just moved through it. She didn't pretend it wasn't there. She felt it. She cried when it hurt. And then she went right back to coloring, asking for more chips, taking each moment as it came.

Ellie was suffering; there was no denying that. She felt the nausea, the fevers, the pricks from needles, the exhaustion. She knew, in her own way, that something about her life was very different from other kids'. She wore masks around strangers, couldn't run to the playground, heard Emily and I worrying about every stray germ. She might not have had the words for it, but she knew something was amiss.

She just didn't dwell on it. She carried on, in spite of everything. She found a way to stay in the moment.

I hadn't invented anything new with my framework. I was just remembering something we all know before life wears it down: acceptance isn't giving up. It's seeing what's true, then acting. It's carrying on. It's doing the right thing anyway. It's asking "Now what?" and taking the next step forward.

Ellie didn't need a framework for that. But I did. And that was okay. The best teacher I had was sitting right inside the hospital room with me, legs dangling happily from the bed, thrilled to get some extra TV time.

I couldn't make Ellie's fever disappear. I couldn't undo her diagnosis. But I could be there with her, in the moment, with the same calm and acceptance she already modeled. I could make choices, one at a time, that made space for the next moment, and the next after that.

I wasn't advocating for some spontaneous, whimsical approach to life's twists and turns. I wasn't downplaying the severity of a cancer diagnosis or abandoning my responsibility to care about Ellie's future. Those fears never went away completely, nor should they have.

Instead, it was the awareness that both mindsets could coexist. The fear could sit there, in the passenger seat, but didn't have to drive. The worry could whisper its what-ifs, but it didn't get to make the final call. In the face of so much we couldn't control, there was still always something we could do next. Sometimes, that meant taking a deep breath and steadying my pulse after a stressful lab result. Other times, it meant helping Ellie choose which flavor ice cream she wanted for dessert.

Keeping the fear quiet in the passenger seat didn't mean pretending it wasn't there. It meant refusing to let it take the wheel. It wasn't a switch that was flipped overnight: it was a daily, deliberate practice, training my mind to find something steady to stand on.

Routines became my anchor, the stable ground beneath the chaos. If the rest of my life was going to be flooded with questions and unknowns, I could build certainty in small, dependable ways.

Every morning, I woke up at 5:00 a.m. I made coffee the same way, in the same mug, and sat on the same spot on the couch. Before the sunrise, before the house stirred, I quietly read books. Nonfiction ignited my curiosity; fiction carried me somewhere else entirely. Both were an antidote to fear, test results, and chemo schedules. When my mind was in the pages before me, it couldn't drift elsewhere.

I doubled down on my own physical and mental wellbeing. I lifted weights. I ran. I sat in the sauna and sweated out the worst of my anxieties. I ate better, prepped meals, and tracked calories. I kept up with doctors appointments preventatively. I scheduled recurring blood work, DEXA scans, and check ups.

When Marcus Aurelius insisted that we have power over our minds, the 'power' he spoke of needed to be trained. Routines became my training ground. They were proof that even in life's most unpredictable moments, there was always something I could strengthen, somewhere I could learn.

Those small, repeatable rituals told my mind: *You are still here. You are still standing. This will not break you. You will get stronger.*

Routine didn't make leukemia disappear, but it gave me a place to stand when the storms came. Because they always came.

No matter how many books I read or weights I lifted, the truth was that cancer didn't care about my schedule or my stoicism. Ellie's fever, sudden hospital stays, and nights pacing down sterile hallways waiting for a doctor's update never went away.

In 2023, Ellie spent nearly 100 days in a hospital or clinic.

And yet, each time, my framework held. It wasn't perfect, but it was just enough. When the fear tried to claw its way back into the driver's seat, I had somewhere to put it. Routine didn't fix chaos, but it kept it from consuming me.

A common misconception about Stoicism is that it calls for the absence of emotion. To be a Stoic, critics say, it to feel nothing. But that's not it at all. Stoicism isn't about becoming emotionless; it's about learning not to be ruled by emotion. It's the difference between feeling fear and acting out of fear, between acknowledging grief and being consumed by it. The Stoics never said "Don't feel." They said, "Feel fully, but don't let those feelings steer the ship."

The mental framework I practiced and the routines I built became the daily exercise of Stoicism itself. They were an ongoing effort to respond with reason when emotion demanded otherwise.

In the months ahead, that philosophy would be tested over and over again.

May of 2023 was, unquestionably, the most challenging and painful part of Ellie's treatment. She developed severe mouth sores, a brutal but not uncommon side effect of certain chemotherapy drugs. This wasn't just a spot or two inside her cheeks; there were dozens of raw, inflamed sores coating her gums, tongue, and throat.

Ellie hardly ate for weeks. We blended smoothies and meal replacement shakes, cheering her on for every sip. She didn't speak more than a few words per day because of the pain. The weight fell off her tiny frame. Her energy dwindled until she spent most of her time curled up on the couch, half awake, cocooned in blankets and pain.

Each morning and night, we still had to brush her teeth. Of all the hardships, this felt the most cruel. I'd hold her chin gently in my palm, guiding the toothbrush across each tender tooth while tears slid down her cheeks. I'd tuck her in bed afterwards and whisper, "I love you," and she'd hum it back to me, lips pressed closed to spare herself the pain.

There's no amount of philosophical wisdom that could dull the ache of seeing your child suffer like that. There is no hidden meaning, no divine silver lining, no comforting metaphysical justification for the pain Ellie had to endure. It just *was*.

For the first time since her diagnosis, Ellie started to *look* like she had cancer. In June, we started noticing long strands of her curly, red hair clinging to the hairbrush after each shower. We knew this would happen, felt the inevitability of it creeping with each clinic appointment. We thought we were prepared for it. But nothing truly prepares you for the moment you run your fingers through your daughter's hair and come away with a handful of it.

Within weeks, the hair that once bounced around her shoulders was gone. She was the same Ellie - sweet, strong, impossibly resilient - but now the world could see her illness before she even said a word.

It started with subtle glances at the grocery store and the puzzled expressions from other kids. There was the time a stranger, seeing only her bald head, referred to Ellie as "he." Even friends and family who knew of Ellie's diagnosis now wore a different kind of expression when she toddled over to say hello. There was a flash of pity, an awkward searching for the right words.

Cancer had always been there, lurking in the body of a beautiful, innocent little girl. But before her hair fell out, the leukemia was invisible. To the outside world, it almost didn't feel real. The clinic visits, the mouth sores, and the transfusions were *our* normal, but no one else saw it. People could only look at her and believe, just for a moment, that everything was fine.

But now they couldn't look away. Now there was a child in a size 4T dress with hearts and unicorns on it, standing quietly in front of them with no hair. The reality of cancer - its rawness, its randomness, its unfairness - was suddenly impossible to ignore.

But we didn't want pity. Cancer didn't define Ellie, and it didn't define our family either. The glances in our direction weren't meant to be cruel or condescending, but they were still unfair. We just wanted to be normal.

Ellie deserved to be treated like any other three or four year old kid, not like a symbol of tragedy. She had her whole life ahead of her. This diagnosis was a speed bump, not a car wreck.

I wanted people to look past her bald head and hospital bracelets and see the incredible, beautiful, wildly talented little girl we were so lucky to call our daughter. She was more than the diagnosis, more than the hair she lost. I needed the world to see that.

When Ellie lost her hair, I braced myself for how it might break her spirit. But she didn't flinch. She shrugged it off the same way she shrugged off the bruises on her arm or the nightly medications. She said that the medicine made her sick hair go away so that new, healthy hair can grow back once her leukemia went away. It never once bothered her.

Watching Ellie respond to those changes changed me, too. It gave me permission to stop wasting energy worrying about how strangers looked at her, or what questions they might ask, or what assumptions they'd make about our family.

If Ellie could stand there, bald and as beautiful as ever in her favorite unicorn dress, then what right did I have to cling to my own hang ups about pity and misunderstanding?

Ellie's courage made it easier for me to talk about her diagnosis calmly, to meet strangers' stares with grace instead of resentment. It wasn't my job to soften her reality or explain it away. My only role was to support her freely.

That didn't mean pretending cancer wasn't there. It meant letting Ellie define how she faced it, day by day, on her own terms. I just needed to follow her lead.

Without question, the world would see her courage and resilience. My job was to make sure she could keep showing it.

Slowly, I felt a sense of purpose building. My beliefs, or lack thereof, hadn't changed over the decades. I didn't find meaning by looking the heavens, I found it in the moments I was living day to day. I found purpose in showing up, holding Ellie's hand, or gently brushing her teeth. It was a quieter, sturdier, personal purpose that shunned cosmic or divine answers and instead focused on the here and now. I found purpose in endurance.

Many talk about cancer like it is a war. They use language like "battles" and "holding the line" or "pushing through." But Ellie taught me something else: endurance could look entirely different. It could be soft, flexible, even joyful. Endurance could be found in her giggles on days she could barely eat, in her twirls on the days she could hardly dance, and her shrug when someone mistook her for a boy.

Her mindset was as remarkable as it was unyielding: *this is who I am today, and that's okay.*

Ellie embodied what it meant to maximize each moment. She was the living definition of 'this happened, now what?' Intentional or not, she had already mastered the Stoic art of governing her own mind and not fixating on what lay beyond her control.

So I stopped searching for some grand, redemptive arc in all of this. I stopped asking 'why us?' and started asking better questions: *What now? What matters? What kind of father do I want to be in this moment?*

When Ellie was first diagnosed, it felt like the ground had been pulled out from under everything I believed. I tried to rebuild certainty piece by piece, in the routines I built or the habits I formed. And to a degree, it worked. Those things helped me stay upright when the world tilted. But they could only take me so far. What I needed beyond was humility to accept what I couldn't fix, curiosity to keep learning through it, and love to hold it all together. The world wouldn't start making sense, but that was never the point. Meaning isn't something to uncover. It's something to create. By living fully in each moment, I was starting to do just that.

9
The Scarf

It's 9:00 a.m. in a hospital room in Charlotte, and Ellie is using a small wooden spoon to scoop vanilla ice cream from the cup on the breakfast tray. I can hear the soft scrape of wood against plastic, a sound that tells me there's nothing left to scoop. She lifts the cup to her lips and drinks the last few drops like it's the final dessert on Earth.

If you asked her, maybe randomness in the universe isn't so bad after all. She's having ice cream for breakfast. What's there to complain about?

"Best. Morning. Ever." she giggles, wiping her lips with the back of her hand.

By July, we had already visited the hospital or clinic over 40 times in 2023. Some were planned for chemotherapy infusions, lab work, or routine check ins. Others, like this one, came out of no where. Ellie had caught some sort of virus just days before 4th of July. While the rest of the country was prepping for barbecues and fireworks, we were waiting for Ellie's neutrophil count to stabilize.

During these unplanned stays, we abandoned the usual parenting rules. Screen time limits disappeared. So did most expectations around meals. And yes, breakfast was sometimes ice cream.

In the face of so much unpredictability, these small rituals like dessert for breakfast, her favorite cartoon, or her glittery unicorn slippers became their own kind of order. We had traded in a routine built around play time and naps for one built around vital checks and anti-nausea medication. Yet somehow, Ellie still found the rhythm in it. She didn't need normal. She needed presence. And sometimes, she just needed ice cream.

The summer of 2023 was a rollercoaster of extremes. We lived through the highest highs and the lowest lows. Ellie was responding to treatment as expected and in some ways, even better than expected. But that promising long-term outlook came at a steep cost: pain and distress in the here and now.

We had entered the phase of treatment known as Delayed Intensification. This stage meant to eliminate any lingering leukemia cells and, more critically, reduce the risk of relapse. For Ellie, that meant enduring an aggressive and exhausting medication regimen that pushed her small body to its limits.

The names alone were dizzying: methotrexate, dexamethasone, Rylaze, Septra, Levaquin, Cytoxan, and more. Some were administered at the clinic, but most became part of our daily life at home. Every morning and night, Emily would line up the medications on the kitchen counter, carefully counting the milliliters. Ellie would trudge over reluctantly, but she never complained.

We had already witnessed her strength in countless ways, but the quiet resolve she showed with her medications was something else entirely. Her bravery wasn't loud or dramatic. It was steady, unshakable, and constant. It was the daily reminder that even on the hardest days, Ellie was still showing up and still shining through it all.

This was most evident with the at home treatment that couldn't be administered orally. For several weeks, we had to give Ellie chemotherapy injections in her leg. At just three years old, she would calmly sit on our couch and look away as the needle pierced her skin.

She cried quietly the first time. But after that? Not a word of protest. Not even a flinch.

It was one of the hardest things we've ever had to do. Each day, we'd hold her tiny leg steady, knowing the pain it would bring. And yet, she bore it with a quiet strength that left us stunned. Her resilience wasn't just inspiring, it was humbling.

Emily, too, carried a mental toughness that cannot be understated. She was the one who gave most of the injections. She never hesitated, never passed on the responsibility, even when I offered. She just did what needed to be done.

Each time, she'd put on a calm, steady face for Ellie and went through the motions: prepping the syringe, checking the dosage, gently pressing the disinfectant solution to Ellie's leg.

Being the one to hurt your child, even for its sake of healing, chips away at you in ways that are hard to explain. We did it because we had to, because we loved Ellie more than anything. Though we always led with softness and gentle care, moments like these demanded something else: a steely, unflinching presence that focused solely on execution.

Whatever pain the needles caused paled in comparison to the side effects of chemotherapy. Mouth sores and loss of hair were excruciating enough, but they were only the beginning. Ellie endured constant bone and muscle pain, paired with crushing fatigue. When other kids were running through playgrounds or tumbling through gymnastics classes, we sometimes celebrated Ellie making it from the couch to the bathroom on her own.

But little by little, her condition was improving, her body showing the same resilience as her mind. One night before bedtime, she insisted on climbing up the stairs to her room by herself. For weeks, she'd asked to be carried because her legs simply hurt too much.

I watched her small frame move with careful determination, one step at a time. She clutched the handrail, wincing as she lifted each leg, waving away my offers to help. When she reached the top, her smile lit up the hallway.

"Daddy! I was able to climb up the stairs all by myself!" she beamed. "I'm getting better!"

As a parent, it was both gutting and uplifting all at once. I knew how monumental this moment was, how much effort and pain had gone into those few steps. But watching her recognize it too was something else entirely. She was beginning to grasp the gap between what she once couldn't do and what she just had.

We never hid Ellie's diagnosis or her condition from her. She knew she had leukemia. She understood what was happening to her body, even if only in the way a three year old could. From the early days in the hospital in New Jersey, we chose honesty. Not cruelty, but clarity. We didn't lie or sugarcoat what was coming. We owed her that much: to tell her the truth and to walk through it all together.

At times, she embraced it. She wore her diagnosis like a badge of honor, proudly telling people how brave she was and how much stronger she was getting. Other times, she saw the injustice of it all, even if her three year old mind simply couldn't make sense of it yet.

Summer amplified that injustice. Most days, we couldn't visit the local playgrounds or the neighborhood pool. Birthday parties, play dates, and sleepovers had to be turned down, no matter how much she wanted to go. Her immune system was often nonexistent. A cough or sneeze from another child on the jungle gym could land her in the hospital for a week.

As a parent, it was excruciating. Free play, social connection, and exploration make up the foundations of childhood. They're how kids learn who they are in the world. But when those essential things come with extraordinary risk, you're forced into impossible choices. We had to choose the lesser evil: safety over normalcy, health over joy. And even when we made the right choice, it never felt like a victory.

Even when we did everything right, the hardest part was how unpredictable it all was.

One day Ellie would be full of energy, dancing in the living room and making up songs about her favorite stuffed animals. The next, she could barely lift her head off the pillow in the morning. The medication dictated the rhythm in her days; it stole away her autonomy.

Chemotherapy wasn't just harsh, it was erratic. Some mornings, Ellie would eat a dozen pancakes and ask me to play with her right after. Other mornings, she'd crawl to the couch in silence, wincing at each step, her body too sore or her stomach too nauseous to do much of anything.

We never knew which version of Ellie we were going to get. More unfairly, neither did she.

That unpredictability wore on all of us. It blurred the line between progress and setback, between joy and pain. Every small victory was followed by the quiet dread of an upcoming crash. But in between those highs and lows, something else was taking shape; it was a quiet resilience, a kind of emotional muscle memory. We were learning, slowly, to ride the waves.

We built our days around those waves. On those slower, heavier ones, we'd prepare her favorite soup and set up makeshift coloring stations beside the sofa. Crayons, stickers, and half-finished drawings covered our living room like offerings to normalcy. On better days, we made the most of them however we could. Sometimes, that meant pulling the bikes out of the garage so that Ellie could feel the sun on her face. Other days, it meant celebrating when Ellie managed to eat a full meal.

Eventually, we learned the rhythm of her medications like a second language. We could anticipate when the nausea would hit, when the steroids would spark ravenous hunger or sudden mood swings, when her energy would fade. Even her cravings became predictable. One week it was smoothies for every meal; the next, Belgian waffles by the dozen. We joked that she'd soon qualify for dual citizenship in Belgium.

Yet even with that structure, we were always ready for the unexpected. Overnight bags lined the garage doors, packed and repacked with clothes, snacks, and toys for the next hospital stay. We didn't wait for emergencies anymore. We planned for them. Cancer created that strange paradox: everything was unpredictable, yet everything was prepared for.

As the summer heat began to give way to the first hints of fall, Ellie herself became a paradox. Physically, she still bore all the markings of a child in treatment. Her hair had just begun to grow back but still left her nearly bald. She had lost several pounds from her already tiny frame, her body fragile and pale from chemotherapy.

But underneath what the world could see, there were glimmers of progress. We were beginning to get our Ellie back.

The rhythm we had built over the summer - the routines, the couch days, the art stations - had created a kind of fragile normal. And within that normal, Ellie began to shine brighter.

One Saturday, we spent hours in the backyard blowing bubbles. I didn't realize how much I missed the sound of her laughter echoing across the lawn until I heard it again. She sat in a patio chair, blowing bubbles toward Rosie and shrieking with delight as Rosie chased them, snapping at the air. Her laughter was wild and unfiltered, untouched by steroids or fatigue. For a moment, she wasn't a child with cancer. She was just a child.

She may have looked sick, but that moment felt like the first real glimpse of light at the end of the tunnel. And for the first time in a long time, I allowed myself to imagine what life *after* leukemia might feel like.

Of course, that tunnel was still long. We still had over a year of treatment left, and we knew better than to get too comfortable. But moments like that afternoon in the yard reminded us that Ellie was still in there, full of joy, mischief, and wonder. We just had to create the right conditions to let her out.

So when the opportunity came for her to serve as the honorary captain at a Charlotte F.C. soccer match, we hesitated for only a moment. There was some risk. Her immune system was still recovering and crowds meant exposure. But her counts were stable and emotionally, she needed it. We all did.

Doctors gave Ellie the all-clear and the date was set. I was absolutely thrilled. A lifelong soccer fan and devoted supporter of the local team, I couldn't have been prouder. But more than that, I just wanted her to have fun. I wanted her to be a normal kid, even if just for a night.

What followed was one of the most unexpectedly beautiful days of our lives.

Charlotte F.C. has a tradition before each match: the roads around the stadium are shut down, and fans march uptown together. The sound of drums, trumpets, and thousands of voices singing fills the streets. It's a triumphant procession toward the pitch, an entire city moving as one. Every fan is decked out in jerseys, hats, and most iconically, scarves.

The tradition of the soccer scarf dates back to early 1900s England. Matches were played outdoors, rain or shine, through the cold fall and winter months. Fans knit wool scarves in their team's colors to keep warm. By the 1950s and 60s, as televised matches became common, scarves evolved. Fans began raising them above their heads while singing anthems and celebrating goals. Over time, the scarf became a symbol of identity, pride, and community.

Today, that tradition spans the globe. Major League Soccer clubs design elaborate, one-of-a-kind scarves to commemorate each season or special matches. They've become universal emblems of belonging.

For Ellie's honorary captaincy, she was asked to design her own scarf. She drew a pattern of brightly colored rainbows, soccer balls, and smiley faces, bookended by the team logo on either side. We figured we might get to keep a few as keepsakes for family and friends.

Instead, we watched in awe as thousands of fans flowed through the stadium wearing *her* scarf. An entire crowd of adults, children, families were wrapped in Ellie's creation. The rainbows and smilies she drew spread across the stands like a living mural of support.

Ellie was stunned. The first time she saw someone wearing it, she gasped and shouted, "I made that scarf!" Every few steps, she'd point and yell, "Look! They have one too!" The magic didn't wear off the entire night.

Not a single ball was kicked yet, and it was already the best night of her life.

As we made our way to our seats, Ellie's joy could barely be contained. She had her scarf wrapped proudly around her neck, a hot dog in one hand, and ice cream on the way. She radiated pure, unfiltered happiness.

As the players were warming up before the game, a team staff member invited us down toward the field. As honorary captain, Ellie would present the match ball to the officials, just a few feet from the pitch.

Ellie was buzzing with excitement as we watched the players warm up. "Daddy, look!" She said, pointing at the field, "that's *really* them!"

We were close enough to hear the players' pre-game chatter and the feel the mist from the sprinklers priming the grass. When the players finished warming up, Ellie got to high-five each one. Her eyes were wide and her smile stretched from ear to ear.

As the last player walked off, she turned to me and asked, "Daddy, can I run on the field and kick the ball?"

I glanced at the staff member, who grimaced and tilted her head apologetically. Stepping onto the pitch was off-limits; every blade of grass was meticulously maintained for play. Still, I had to try.

I made my case, Ellie's hopeful eyes doing most of the work. The woman sighed, then grinned. "She's got 60 seconds after they announce her captaincy. But you didn't hear that from me."

I mouthed a 'thank you' and crouched beside Ellie. The announcer's voice boomed across the stadium as her face lit up on the jumbotron. He shared our family's story while 30,000 fans rose to their feet, scarves held high, cheering for Ellie. I leaned down and said, "Okay, run!"

Ellie grabbed the ball from the podium and sprinted toward midfield. The fastest player on the team couldn't have caught her if he tried. She dribbled the ball with the joy of a child and the focus of a pro, giggling all the way. It was the happiest I had seen her since the diagnosis.

The crowd erupted. Fans cheered, clapped, and called her name. I stood frozen, watching it all unfold. I didn't realize I was crying until I saw it on the big screen.

The emotion hit me like a wave. This moment, this gesture, this impossibly strong kid, was at the center of it all. It was the proudest I'd ever been.

But it wasn't just pride. It was meaning. This was what I wanted the world to see. Yes, no child deserves what Ellie has endured. Yes, the last year has been chaos beyond imagination. But no one needed to feel sorry for us. They just needed to be with us in that moment.

Because we're still here. We're still standing. In this one beautiful, electric moment, Ellie was doing more than that. She was flying, ball at her feet, laughter in the air, a stadium behind her.

We didn't need sorrow. We needed the world to see Ellie for who she truly was.

The fireworks that lit up the Charlotte skyline before kickoff didn't shine half as brightly as Ellie did that night. As we made our way back to our seats, she was met with high fives at every step, each supporter treating her like part of the team.

It was nearly 8:00 p.m., Ellie's usual bedtime, but there was no way we were calling it a night.

Ellie stood for most of the match, cheering every goal, groaning dramatically at near-misses, and dancing to every song that pulsed through the stadium. By the end, she stood tall with her scarf raised high, just like the thousands of other fans around her.

The match. The scarf. That night. It transcended the sport.

It became something much more.

It became a moment of healing. A night where happiness outshined fear. A place where Ellie wasn't a patient, she was just a kid. Strangers became teammates in her story, lifting her up not out of pity, but in celebration.

It was proof that even in the middle of something unimaginably hard, beauty can still break through.

That night, after the noise faded and the lights dimmed, I carefully set Ellie's scarf on her nightstand and tucked her into bed.

"The game was a tie, right?" she asked, her voice soft and sleepy but still alive with excitement.

I nodded.

She smiled. "Then can we go back? Maybe if I go on the field again, I can score a goal so we can win."

I smile and kissed her forehead. "I bet you could score a goal on that field."

She yawned and shrugged, "Of course I can. I was so fast."

And there it was: Ellie in her purest form. Unshaken, unbothered, and still dreaming. Always looking ahead, still believing that the next time might be different, might be better. Even in exhaustion, she was already plotting her return, ready to make the most out of whatever moment came next.

I gently closed her bedroom door and glanced at my phone for the first time in hours. The screen lit up with missed calls and messages from friends and family celebrating Ellie's night.

Local news outlets had shared clips of Ellie running onto the field. Her honorary captaincy was highlighted at length, including several interviews with Emily and me sharing her story. One anchor even wore Ellie's scarf proudly on-air, calling it "a small token to celebrate one amazing little girl."

We were also able to publicly recognize the doctors and nurses who made nights like this possible. It felt right to turn the spotlight toward them, too. So many of Ellie's brightest moments were guided by their steady hands, clear minds, and open hearts. There is no version of that evening without the support of the hospital staff. There would be no scarf held high, no field sprint, and no laughter echoing through the stadium without them.

Those doctors and nurses had seen Ellie on her hardest days. They were the ones who gently persuaded her to try the French toast when she wouldn't eat, nudged her out of bed when she couldn't find the strength, and made her laugh when the world seemed too heavy for a three year old to carry. Most importantly, they never stopped seeing her as a little girl first and a patient second.

They memorized her favorite songs, knew exactly how to distract her when the IV line wouldn't cooperate, and learned to read her moods and anticipate her needs when we couldn't. They adjusted medications, stayed late, called us after hours, and even celebrated every bit of progress as if it was their own child's.

And it wasn't just Ellie they cared for. They gave Emily and me grace when were exhausted or scared or asking the same questions for the fifth time that night. They were transparent and kind, hard-working and gentle handed. They didn't see us as the parents of a cancer patient. They saw us as parents.

That night, the game was broadcast live on every television in the hospital. I imagined nurses and doctors in the pediatric oncology unit clapping along with the supporters in the stands, shedding similar tears when Ellie sprinted onto the field.

It wasn't just our moment. It was theirs, too.

That night wasn't just a milestone for us. It was a shared victory. A small but shining reminder that hope can still find its way through even the darkest places.

10
Silly Questions

Moments like that night at the stadium didn't just happen. They were the product of intention, of choosing again and again to build something beautiful in the middle of chaos. And not just for Ellie, but for anyone watching. It was a night built on presence, perspective, and preparation.

We were still more than a year away from the end of Ellie's treatment. That night couldn't erase any past hardship or prevent us from those yet to come. We still carried fear, still lived in the shadow of lab results and uncertainty. But nights like that reminded me that beauty and hardship don't cancel each other out. They coexist. The more fully we allowed both, the more vivid life became.

My role as a parent, as a husband, and as a friend is to stay in the arena. To show others that we can participate in joy when it shows up and make the most of the moments when it doesn't. To hold the perspective that even amid the chaos, we are still profoundly fortunate.

Philosophy may have given me the language for this, but fatherhood taught me to speak it. To live it.

Stoicism says, "the obstacle is the way." I used to read that as a metaphor: what seems to block the path is actually the way forward. Every hardship is an invitation to build character, discipline, and endurance. I had a poster of some lone figure climbing a mountain, wind in their face, looking determined.

But now, I know. It's not a metaphor. It's life.

There is no obstacle-free path. We all carry a weight of some kind. Some are born with a two-ton weight strapped to their shoulders; others accumulate still heavier stones over time. What defines us isn't the weight itself, but how we carry it. It's how we keep moving through the terrain that challenges us.

It's tempting to ask why those obstacles are there. Why this? Why me? Why now? But those questions don't move us forward. They trap us in the past. They promise understanding when what we need is direction.

We tell ourselves that if we could just understand the 'why,' the climb would be easier. That if we could extract meaning from the mountain, the suffering would feel justified. But not all questions are helpful ones.

Richard Dawkins, one of the most influential evolutionary biologists of our time, was once asked the timeliness question in of "why." His answer was sharp:

"To the question 'Why do mountains exist?' - you could give an answer in terms of the geological processes that give rise to mountains - but that's not what you want. You want something about the purpose of mountains.

'What is the purpose of a mountain?' It's a silly question. It doesn't deserve an answer. The correct answer is 'don't ask such a silly question.'"

And yet, it's in our nature to ask.

We all face mountains. Some rise up in front of us suddenly, others over years. We name them, plan our routes, and often whisper to ourselves, "Why this one? Why now?"

When pressed on whether it's simply human nature to ask such questions, Dawkins didn't waver:

"It may well be part of the human condition to ask silly questions."

I admire Dawkins' dismissiveness. It's blunt, but productive. There's a deeper truth in that British wit. Those "why" questions, disguised as philosophy, often paralyze us. We want the universe to justify itself, to make our suffering mean something. We want the mountain to have a purpose. We crave meaning amongst the boulders.

But the truth is, the mountain doesn't care if we climb it. There's no divine inscription carved into the stone, no secret waiting at the summit. The mountain simply *is*.

Meaning, though, is still possible. But it's not discovered, it's created. Not given, but built. And it begins not with "why," but with "how."

How do I show up on the mountain? How will I breathe when the air thins? How can I keep my footing when the rocks shift beneath me? How can I hold onto hope when the summit disappears in the fog? How can I prepare for the next one?

Notice that these questions don't concern themselves with outside events. They don't chase after reasons or justifications behind the uncontrollable randomness of the universe. Instead, they shift the gaze inward. They don't prepare the mind for the 'why;' they focus only what's in front of us and what comes next. They are interested in what's in our control. They are rooted in presence and forward motion, navigating the trail underfoot and the climb ahead.

Before takeoff, airlines remind us: secure your own oxygen mask before helping others. These 'how' questions do the same. They oxygenate the mind. They ground it in self-awareness and immediate action.

And in moments of hardship, this shift from external causes to internal agency does more than just ease the mind. It restores a sense of autonomy. It says: *you can still choose how to climb.*

Of course, not everyone finds that internal agency or purpose sufficient. Some argue that without a higher power, an afterlife, or some deeper metaphysical meaning in life, internal meaning is merely a placeholder - a temporary comfort in the face of ultimate meaningless. If there is no deity, they'd ask, then what's the point? One day, we were born and on another, we will die. Why assign personal meaning to something so random, so temporary, so inevitably doomed to end?

That line of thinking is as shortsighted as it is misinformed.

Right now, I am sitting in my house, writing this book. Decades ago, this house didn't exist. One day in the future, it will be gone. Like life, it is here for a finite period of time. No more, no less.

But none of that stops me from loving this place, from creating memories here, from making it a home. The impermanence of this home doesn't diminish its meaning. In fact, it enhances it.

If, at the moment of my death, I somehow learn there's nothing beyond this life, then so be it. I don't *need* a higher purpose or power to justify this life or this home. I live here, now. My task is to make the most of it. To choose how I'll face each day within its walls. That autonomy begins with how I prepare my mind. My goal is to make it just slightly better than it was yesterday, to infuse it with a little more steadiness, clarity, and compassion.

Meaning isn't something we discover at the summit of the mountain. It's something we construct, step by step, during the climb.

Asking "why" can become its own form of suffering. It suggests that pain is purposeful, that there's a hidden order behind cruelty, or that we somehow earned what happened to us. The question assumes there's an answer waiting to be discovered, one that could make it all make sense. But that search can twist inward, turning grief into guilt, and curiosity into torment. Some things don't have a reason that justifies them. And trying to force one only deepens the wound.

No one deserves to find themselves on the mountain that our family has climbed. Ellie never asked for that mountain to appear so that some deeper purpose could be revealed. Had leukemia never entered our lives, we would've found another purpose elsewhere. This wasn't destiny. It wasn't divine intervention. The genetic error that tossed our lives into chaos was as random as it was without intent.

So, we didn't ask why. We asked how. How can we make the most of this moment? How can we retain our autonomy by asking: *This happened. Now what?* How can we find a purpose in that?

I was beginning to find that personal purpose that felt honorable, but it still needed refining. Early on in Ellie's treatment, I mistook that autonomy for isolation. I believed the pursuit of "now what?" was a mission I had to undertake alone. My family was suffering, and I thought it was my job to fix it. That was all I knew.

But mountains are rarely climbed alone.

Somewhere along the way, I realized that I wasn't alone on this trail. The strength to keep climbing often came from those climbing alongside me. It's easy to believe that resilience is forged in solitude, but more often, it's reinforced in connection. We didn't get through this because *I* was strong. We got through this because *we* were. Because Emily was the most incredible mother and wife on the planet. Because our family, friends, and community climbed with us.

No matter how strong the body, mind, and heart are, we still rely on one another to keep climbing. Sometimes, that support looked like 30,000 people in a soccer stadium. Other times, it was the quiet text from a friend that says, "I'm thinking about you." Or the gentle voice of a nurse who softly says "You are great parents." Support didn't always roar like the Charlotte F.C. fans; sometimes, it whispered.

Our climb was filled with moments where that whisper kept us going.

There were family members who dropped everything to help with logistics, and friends who made us laugh when we didn't think we could. Nights spent in the emergency room with Ellie, knowing Rosie was sleeping soundly at my sister's house. Each act, no matter how small, became part of the scaffolding that held us up. We didn't carry the weight alone. It was shared, quietly and beautifully redistributed in ways we didn't always recognize at the time.

But of all of the people who showed up for Ellie, no one stood taller than Emily.

Emily carried the weight of appointments, medications, sleepless nights, endless hospital paperwork, insurance phone calls, and the thousand invisible decisions that come with being a mother to a child with cancer. She did it all while protecting the sanctity of Ellie's childhood. Even on the hardest days, she found ways to make Ellie laugh. She kept her smiling. She kept us all standing.

I learned from Emily that real endurance is about presence. It's about showing up, over and over again, even when you're exhausted, even when you're scared, even when there's no finish line in sight.

Our marriage, already strong as can be, somehow grew even stronger through Ellie's treatment. We each found a personal purpose in the pain: *If we can get through this, then we can get through anything. Together.*

But it wasn't easy.

There were nights we didn't speak. It wasn't out of anger, but because we had no words left. And mornings when a tired glance said everything that needed to be said. Somehow, that was enough. We were living through each other's worst nightmare, but we were still in it together. Side by side.

That became our strength. It was a bond that couldn't be shaken. A respect rooted not just in love, but in the understanding of what each other was carrying. And the tools we brought to the trail to keep climbing, together.

We communicated clearly and constantly, never hiding how we felt. We were transparent around what *could* happen and what needed to. We shared our frustrations and our fears, our anxiety and our hope. We were open about our need for space or togetherness. We never held grudges, recognizing that bigger battles were unfolding all around us.

Most importantly, we shared one unshakeable belief: Ellie *would* make it through this as long as we were side by side.

And we weren't alone in that belief.

Toward the end of 2023, Ellie had even more and more chances to show the world her strength. That fall, she was invited to participate in a fashion show supporting pediatric cancer research. It was a glamorous affair: long gowns, celebrity guests, a multi-course dinner, and a dazzling, chandelier-lit ballroom. Ellie's part was simple: she'd walk on the runway with one of the featured celebrities and strut her stuff for the crowd. A sixty second walk. That's all it was meant to be.

At least, on paper.

Backstage, Ellie was nervous. The lights, the noise, the crowd, the idea of walking in front of all those people suddenly felt huge. We held her hand in the makeshift greenroom and talked her through what it would be like. At first, she wasn't having it. She laid back on the couch, arms crossed, and didn't budge when we asked if she wanted to practice her walk.

Then, a volunteer makeup artist walked into the room. Her bag was filled with colorful makeup and props that immediately caught Ellie's attention.

"Hi, is Ellie available?" she asked, kneeling down with a big smile.

Ellie peeked up from the couch, still skeptical, but curious.

"I've got sparkles, face paint, glitter, bows, you name it. What's your favorite color?"

Slowly, Ellie sat up, then scooted forward to look in the bag. Within minutes, she was perched in the makeup chair, completely locked in. The nervousness didn't vanish, but it dissipated with every sparkle of glitter added to Ellie's cheek. The makeup artist handed her a mirror and Ellie beamed at her reflection: just enough playful makeup to feel magical but still very much herself.

That moment flipped a switch.

Ellie jumped from the chair and strutted confidently up and down the greenroom floor, giggling with joy. She twirled in her pink, fluffy dress and proudly adjusted the bow on the headband. In those moments, she wasn't thinking about the hair she had lost or the chemotherapy appointment waiting later that week. She was just a kid, living out a dream she didn't know she had.

When it came time to walk out, she didn't just step onto the runway. She *owned* it.

She marched beside her celebrity escort, beaming ear to ear. She stopped at the center, struck a pose, and waved to the cheering crowd. With each outfit change, Ellie's confidence grew. Each time she reappeared, her smile widened and her walk turned into a run. This wasn't just a fashion show anymore: it was her playground. The audience erupted every time she took the stage. She was truly putting on a show now, jumping and twirling, blowing kisses like she'd done it a hundred times before.

If there were any lingering doubts that her nerves were gone, the final walk made it crystal clear.

She stepped into her favorite dress and strapped on a pair of wide, colorful butterfly wings. Tiny lights sparked along the wings' edges. The ballroom lights dimmed, and a soft, magical glow surrounded her frame. Ellie looked beautiful.

But there was no slow, sentimental stroll to close the show.

She sprinted down the runway like it was a race, arms stretched wide, wings glowing, joy radiating from every inch of her. When the host stepped out from behind the curtain to deliver the closing remarks, Ellie didn't flinch.

"THE SHOW MUST GO ON!" she exclaimed. She giggled on stage, fully living out the moment and eating up the attention from the crowd. She danced up and down the runway to the music echoing through the ballroom. Two hours earlier, we couldn't get her off the couch. Now, we couldn't get her back on to it.

Emily and I inched toward the runway and finally caught Ellie's eye. We gently coaxed her backstage as the host wrapped up the evening.

People stood, clapped, and wiped tears from their eyes. We did too. Not because of the gowns or the glitter or the celebrity cameos, but because of the strength and courage on display that night.

The event was live-streamed online and captured thousands of viewers across the globe. Family in both New Jersey and North Carolina watched in real time as Ellie ran across the stage. When the fashion show ended, my phone had dozens of alerts from family and friends thoroughly entertained by Ellie's antics. The support was overwhelming, and I was again reminded of just how much love surrounded her every single day.

It wasn't just a fashion show. It was a celebration of these children and all the mountains they had to climb. It was a reminder that, yet again, joy finds a way to burst through even the darkest of moments.

The happiness that Ellie experienced that night didn't appear out of no where. It didn't come because it was earned or manifested or destined. It came because others helped create the conditions for it to emerge. And those conditions had been slowly tilting in our favor as the year drew to a close.

Sometimes, it was Emily coaxing Ellie off the coach after hours of resistance. Other times, it was a volunteer with a face full of glitter and a bag full of magic. Some days, it was the unexpected FaceTime from a friend of family member, or the surprise meal left on our porch. On harder days, it was the nurse who stayed past her shift to make sure Ellie got to sleep without pain. Those moments weren't always as dramatic as the soccer match or the fashion show. They weren't captured in photographs or streamed online. But they were the scaffolding that held up the joy that we so desperately needed.

I've come to think of the people and acts of kindness we experienced as something like gravity.

They're the reason everything stays upright and the force that kept us grounded. They're why we didn't collapse under the weight of the world. It wasn't something we went out looking for or even thought to ask about, but we simply wouldn't have been able to carry on without it. Like gravity disappearing, we would have known immediately if that support wasn't there.

There's a word for this kind of help, though I didn't use it much at the time: grace. Not grace in a religious or spiritual sense, but the strange human phenomenon of receiving care you didn't earn. Of support you didn't request. Of love you couldn't possibly repay.

I never knew how to respond in the moment.

We're all trained to think in transactions. Give and take. Deserve and earn. Quid pro quo. But grace defies that logic. It's a math equation with no equals sign, a formula that doesn't add up. It doesn't care about fairness. It just is.

It arrived whether we deserved it or not, whatever "deserved" meant. It came from loved ones, strangers, and sometimes, from within ourselves. I didn't always recognize it at the time. I was too busy holding our world together with philosophical aphorisms and sheer will. But looking back, it's undeniable: grace was everywhere. It was disproportionately in our favor. Overwhelmingly so.

At times, it was hard to accept.

It was humbling in a way that left me speechless and unsure of what to do with it all. I felt a strange, ever-present guilt creep in when help came our way; an unease born from an equation that didn't balance. Some might call this survivor's guilt. I'm not sure that label fits perfectly, but it's close. It's the discomfort of being loved so deeply, of receiving grace you don't feel like you deserve.

I'd talk to friends, family, even strangers about Ellie's situation and see the pity in their eyes, feel their genuine concern. But I didn't feel like we were the ones who deserved it.

I had walked around hospital halls. I had seen children much sicker than Ellie. I had spoken to parents facing more brutal versions of the same randomness we were living through. Mothers and fathers who would have switched places with us in a heartbeat. Some who would never get to bring their child home.

And some who faced it all completely alone. No visitors. No family. No GoFundMe pages. No one showing up with meals or care packages or gift bags.

They were climbing their own mountains that were higher, colder, and lonelier than ours. We had ropes, gear, and fellow climbers cheering us on. And so, I instinctively started to downplay our own pain. Our mountain was starting to look more like a hill; theirs was Everest.

I had a front row seat to what our lives could have looked like.

When Ellie was diagnosed, I viewed randomness as a cruel, unforgiving fact of *our* world. But over time, that cruelty was put into perspective: we were the lucky ones. We didn't feel fortunate in the moment, but we had so much to be grateful for. The lab results that did come back positive. The future date when Ellie would ring the bell. The day we did walk into our new home as a family.

These are things that other families would never experience. That realization sat heavy. It made every gift harder to accept, every gesture more complicated. Each act of generosity brought questions I couldn't quite answer.

Why were people so generous to us when others needed it more? What kind of person am I to accept this kindness when others are more deserving? How can I attend soccer matches and fashion shows when the child in the room next to ours might never go home?

In the moment, I said "thank you." I returned the hugs, accepted the kindness, and meant every word of it. I could see the beauty in how humanity comes together in crisis.

But beneath that gratitude was a quiet, gnawing tension. There was a sense of injustice I didn't know how to resolve. *Don't worry about us,* I thought. *We'll be fine. Others need it more. Go help them, not us.*

I reflected on grace, support, and kindness often as Thanksgiving 2023 approached. It was going to be the first 'normal' holiday since Ellie's diagnosis just over a year prior. We wanted to mark the occasion by giving back to those that helped us thus far, even if only in some small way. We had a festive family dinner planned with immediate and extended family joining us to celebrate Ellie completing her first year of treatment. For weeks, we took extra precaution to avoid Ellie getting sick before the big day.

But the universe had other ideas. Two days before Thanksgiving, Ellie spiked a fever. Still immunocompromised, she needed another trip to the emergency room.

We arrived at the hospital disheartened and defeated. In all likelihood, this would be the second consecutive Thanksgiving spent in a hospital room. We tried to hide our frustration and contain our concern for Ellie, but it spilled over at every opportunity. Even Ellie was over it.

A nurse came in to check vitals when we arrived. She was typing away at a computer, checking Ellie's temperature and measuring her blood oxygen levels.

I turned to Ellie and asked softly, "Are you doing okay? Do you need anything?"

Ellie, tired and fed up, looked up at the nurse and said, completely deadpan, "The only thing I need is for *someone* to get out of here."

I froze momentarily, unsure whether to laugh hysterically or apologize profusely.

The nurse cracked a smile and that was enough to shatter the tension in the room like glass. Emily and I burst out loud and even Ellie giggled under the blankets. She didn't mean to be rude. Like the rest of us, she had just had enough.

Lab results confirmed that at some point, Ellie contracted RSV. We'd stay at the hospital at least another few days; long enough to cancel Thanksgiving dinner plans.

My parents hosted Thanksgiving dinner, instead. I drove from the hospital to their house to pick up a cooler full of Thanksgiving food to bring to the hospital. Another gracious act that filled me with both gratitude and guilt. On the drive back, I found myself wrestling with the swirl of emotions I couldn't quite name. So I turned back to what had kept me grounded before: Marcus Aurelius's *Meditations*.

There's a Stoic practice called *premeditatio malorum,* or the premeditation of evils. You imagine things going wrong before they happen so you're mentally and emotionally prepared when they do. It's not pessimism; it's a kind of mental rehearsal, a way to cultivate resilience, gratitude, and calm.

The Stoic philosopher Epictetus was blunt about this: "When you kiss your child good night, say to yourself: they make not wake up." (*Discourses,* 3.24)

To someone unfamiliar with Stoicism, that can sound grim, like rehearsing tragedy. But the practice isn't about expecting the worst; it's about defusing the power of fear before it takes hold. By envisioning loss, hardship, or failure in advance, you reduce the shock when life inevitably delivers them.

Seneca called it "immunizing the mind." If you've already pictured the storm, you don't panic when clouds gather. When practiced earnestly, it doesn't drain joy; it intensifies gratitude. Each ordinary moment feels more vivid precisely because you've imagined its absence.

The idea isn't to love less or fear more; it's to love wisely, with eyes open and an awareness of impermanence. It's an acknowledgement of how fragile life is, and by facing that truth, we become both more grateful and less dependent on things staying the same.

That's the paradox of *premeditatio malorum*: by contemplating what could go wrong, you become more present for what's going right. You consider the worst, appreciate when it hasn't come to pass, and strengthen your ability to respond if it ever does.

That practice, and the mindset behind it, gave me a strange kind of clarity. I didn't need to rehearse the worst case scenario. I saw it at every clinic visit. That perspective allowed me to appreciate all that *was* going our way. I was already beginning to feel like we were ready to take on whatever challenges came our way.

But something about that framework still felt incomplete. Like it was missing a final step. If we already felt ready to face what came next, how could we help others who weren't?

As New Year's Day arrived, I started to wonder if maybe I wasn't supposed to balance the scales between grace and guilt. Maybe I was meant to do something with the weight instead. Maybe our family had more to offer.

We might have been the ones receiving support now, but it didn't *always* have to be that way. What if we could give back what we had received, tenfold?

That question stayed with us. It didn't demand an answer right away, but in time, it would reshape how we moved through the world.

It didn't erase the tension between grace and guilt. But it did give us a direction, a vision beyond Ellie's bell-ringing date where we'd be strong enough to lift others. We didn't have to carry grace as a burden; it could be a temporary gift we would later pass on.

With that prospect ahead of us, grace no longer felt like an undeserved reward. Guilt was replaced by motivation.

Grace didn't have to be a reward. It could simply be a reminder that we were seen, loved, and not alone. That motivation became a quiet calling to act with purpose and pay forward what had been so generously given to us.

It wasn't a divine mission. This wasn't about fate. It was a choice. One that, in time, would let us turn gratitude into action.

As 2024 came into view, we weren't just holding on anymore. We were beginning to move forward.

11
Opening Up

Ellie always woke up starving after every lumbar puncture. She wasn't allowed to eat before any procedure, so by the time she came out of the operating room, she had gone what felt like an eternity without food. That sometimes meant no breakfast until midday or later. For a four year old, that might as well be forever.

The moment her eyes opened, before she even knew where she was, she'd croak out the name of the food she wanted. No hesitation. No confusion. Just the exact order of food she demanded within seconds of waking.

Her go-to request was a plain toasted bagel with cream cheese and a cake pop on the side. It became another one of our rituals. On the way to the hospital, we'd stop at a local coffee shop to pickup her post-op meal and hang onto it until she was in recovery.

It gave her a kind of motivation. Whenever she learned she had a lumbar puncture or spinal chemo infusion coming, she'd immediately celebrate the forthcoming cake pop. Like most parents, we tried to limit sweets. But if there's ever a time to make an exception, it's right after chemotherapy.

"Can I...have...my...cake pop?" Ellie asked once, still groggy from the anesthesia. Her eyes were barely open as we handed her the strawberry sprinkle ball of cake and icing. She took small bites, wiping the sleep from her face but savoring each one.

It was early 2024. Things weren't easy, not by a long shot. But they were different. *We* were different.

For the first time since the diagnosis, we felt like we were getting our autonomy back. Though Ellie was still on a full regimen of chemotherapy, she was expected to have longer stretches with a functioning immune system. We were encouraged to get out of the house more, to let her play with other kids, and maybe even plan a family trip somewhere.

Just months before, that had felt unthinkable. But as the new year began, our definition of 'normal' was shifting again. This time, 'normal' for us was moving closer to what 'normal' meant for everyone else.

Returning to that version of normal meant more than stepping back into the outside world physically; it meant returning socially as well. That was both hopeful and foreign. After a year of isolation, reconnecting with people again felt almost like learning to speak a forgotten language.

Contrary to the 'isolationists' stereotype, the Stoics believed humans are inherently social creatures. For them, community wasn't a luxury; it was our nature. We're meant to live with, help, and grow alongside others. Even if it becomes difficult, our duty is to stay connected, not retreat into isolation. Marcus Aurelius detailed this in *Meditations:*

137

"Man by nature is a social animal. If he does not fulfill his social duty, he loses his nature and, if he loses his nature, he is no longer truly a man" (Meditations, 9.9)

I used to read that abstractly, like a philosophical truism. Now it felt deeply personal. Somewhere over the past year, the absence of social life had taken something from me. Without casual conversation, laughter, and the rhythms of everyday interaction, something vital had thinned out. We were living through something enormous, but were trapped inside a tiny bubble. The silence of it all made the suffering both painful and isolating.

The isolation wasn't just a vacuum, it was eroding who we were. Without people to talk to, to laugh with, or even just bump into at the grocery store, something in us began to wear down. We watched our daughters miss out on birthday parties, playdates, and the simple chaos of being kids. But it wasn't just them. We felt it, too. We spent over a year watching friends go on date nights, take trips, and live weekends that didn't orbit around lab results or treatment schedules. Life kept moving for everyone else while ours stayed paused. The distance wasn't only physical. It was emotional, even existential.

We didn't resent our situation. It wasn't about fairness. We knew, without question, that staying home and keeping Ellie safe was the right decision. Ellie's health was always our top priority and that would never change, regardless of how isolated we felt. That's what it means to be a parent.

But that didn't make the loneliness any less real.

Now, with hardest part of treatment behind us, we were finally allowed to be eager and energized about the possibility of real normalcy. Even those once-dreaded procedures began to blend into the routine. They sat on our family calendar alongside dentist appointments and HVAC maintenance reminders. They still carried anxiety, but that anxiety didn't define our lives anymore. After a year of living as a "cancer family," we had learned how to live, period.

We still had more than a year of treatment ahead, but we were ready to reclaim small joys: a morning at the playground or a weekend trip to the mall. To us, it felt like the most freedom we'd had in over a year. Ellie and Rosie could finally have the childhood experiences they deserved.

Emily and I were ready, too. For months, we couldn't go more than a few hours without talking about hemoglobin levels or neutrophil counts. Morning and night, our phone buzzed with chemotherapy reminders and lab updates. But as spring approached, those alerts began to spread apart, like they were making space for a normal life.

We decided to be intentional about reintegrating with the rest of the world. Since we had moved to North Carolina, we hadn't built much of a social network. Now, it felt essential, not optional. Our physical and mental health depended on it.

So we said yes to everything. Emily joined a Sunday morning soccer league, started a neighborhood crafting group, and hosted girls' night dinners. I joined a local Dad's group, attended work happy hours, and played poker with the neighbors once a week. We even saved time for our own date nights, though they often started with reviewing leukemia protocol with my parents before walking out the door.

We were way too excited about having a social life again. After seeing friends, we'd come home acting like we just returned from vacation, buzzing about how good it felt to be out in the world again. It was a reminder that we were human, that we were seen. Our friends knew what we were going through, but it was always an afterthought. We weren't "cancer parents" to them; we were just friends.

Outside of that small circle, though, things still felt different. The shift back toward the rhythms of everyday life meant more time spent out in the world with strangers. And with that came the complicated task of re-engaging socially with people who didn't know our story.

To most, Ellie's short hair said everything before we even opened our mouths. They saw a cancer family. They saw the remnants or something tragic, not the momentum of something hopeful. For us, just being out in public felt like something to celebrate. But to them, we were living in the shadow of something awful. Their glances, softened tones, and sympathetic half smiles weren't malicious or cruel. Everyone meant well. But you could feel the weight of their pity the moment they realized what Ellie was going through.

Ellie felt it, too. As excited as she was for those playground trips, they still came with rules. We hovered near the slide, ready to catch her at any stumble. One fall could mean another trip to the emergency room. Other kids stared just a bit too long at her bald head. Most simply didn't *look* like her. Around us, Ellie never lost her bubbly, friendly personality. But in public, we started noticing something different. It wasn't shame. She never hid or seemed disheartened by her condition. It was more like a cautious awareness, like she knew she was different. And the world around her was subtly reminding her of that.

Looking back, we were all ready to stop being handled so delicately. We didn't want people to tiptoe around us. Our life had changed, but not always in the way people imagined. We weren't living in constant crisis. We weren't waiting for someone to deliver the perfect line of comfort.

And yet, that's often what people tried to do.

Sometimes, it came in the form of a cautious question like "is she okay now?" Or the reflexive, overly optimistic, "Kids are so resilient!" But most often, it came in silence: the awkward pause, the way a room would grow still when her story came up. As if they'd walked into the middle of a tragedy they didn't know how to navigate

How could they?

There are no perfect words to say to a parent whose child is being treated for cancer. We didn't expect anyone to know what to say. *And that was okay.* We didn't hold it against them when they stumbled or avoided the subject altogether. The awkwardness made sense. It didn't anger us. It didn't frustrate us. They didn't need to say anything at all.

Some topics in life are simply too charged or too fragile to talk about easily. Having a child with leukemia is one of them. Of course people would hesitate. Of course they'd be cautious. We never expected comfort to come easily, or for someone to find just the right words to say. We understood and accepted that.

But there *are* wrong things to say. And unfortunately, we heard them all too often. I wish I could say they didn't bother me, that I brushed them off. But that wouldn't be true.

Many of these conversations left me confused, angry, and sometimes resentful.

Almost all of them centered on one idea: that Ellie's suffering was part of a plan. That there was a reason this happened. That the pain had a purpose. That one day we'd understand the silver linings. That it wasn't random. That God works in mysterious ways.

It reminded me of what people said at my grandfather's funeral years earlier. And just like then, none of it helped.

To be clear, the people who said these things meant well. Just like the glances Ellie got at the playground, there was no cruelty behind them. In fact, I believe many truly did find comfort in what they were saying. They believed in a God who allowed this for a reason beyond understanding. They accepted that the explanation was out of reach, but real nonetheless.

So when someone said, "God has a plan for her," or "this is happening to her for a reason," it wasn't just a throwaway platitude. It was a sincere attempt to offer hope. It was an invitation to believe that Ellie's suffering was not meaningless. A reminder that one day, the reason would reveal itself as part of a greater good.

I understand *why* people cling to that. It's a lifeline when hope runs thin. It turns chaos into choreography, pain into purpose. It's a tempting reassurance, especially when the alternative is accepting that sometimes there is no reason. I've reached for that same certainty before, when I couldn't bear to look into the abyss of randomness.

But that framing, however well-intentioned, carries an invisible cost.

It implies that Ellie's pain was necessary. That the hospital beds, the needles, the nausea, and the fear were all meant to happen. It suggests that the suffering of an innocent four year old was a deliberate part of a cosmic plan, an essential variable in some divine equation whose solution we're not allowed to see.

Even if someone truly believes that, it's useless to a parent standing beside their child's hospital bed. In fact, it's more than useless. It's crushing. It rebrands cruelty as design. It turns tragedy into divine intent. And it implies we should be okay with it, because God must have a reason. Because their God is perfect. Because despite what we're seeing, this is love in disguise.

That's the claim: that the suffering of an innocent child isn't an accident of the world, but a feature of it. That God's love somehow requires the existence of pediatric cancer. That the all powerful, all knowing, all benevolent creator of the universe can think of no other way to fulfill his plan than through the agony of a three year old.

Yes, a child is screaming in pain - but fear not, this is God's love in action.

This is about as helpful as telling a drowning man that his lungs were destined to fill with water for a higher purpose. However earnestly offered, these consolations ask for surrender. They ask us to accept obvious evil as part of a higher virtue. And those who offer these generous consolations do so without having to live a single moment of it themselves.

Because they weren't there.

They weren't in my hotel room, a thousand miles away from my daughter. They didn't have to pull the red curls from the hairbrush. They didn't mop up vomit at 2 a.m. for the third night in a row. They didn't hear Ellie's screams of "Please Daddy, help me" when the nurse approached with the catheter. They don't relive those moments. They don't wake from nightmares where Ellie relapses.

If they did, I wonder if they'd still call it God's plan.

The truth is, if a God exists, then he either willed or allowed this. In either case, it means that the world could not be as it should be without Ellie's leukemia. And that suddenly shatters the idea of a wholly good God. Because what kind of moral perfection requires a child's suffering to sustain it?

But of course God is good! Maybe he just didn't *know* Ellie was suffering to that degree. In that case, the image of an omniscient God collapses.

Or maybe he knew, but didn't intend for it to happen. Or maybe once it happened, he couldn't stop it. Or perhaps, for his grand design to unfold, this had to happen. Then he is not all powerful. His supposed "plan" exists beyond his control.

Well, if leukemia is the best he can come up with as a part of his plan, then I don't think that God is a God at all.

Any way you cut it, the notion of an all-knowing, all-powerful, entirely good deity cannot survive this reality. At best, it's comforting fiction. At worst, it's a delusion. It's a refusal to accept that the universe is indifferent and random. It's an unwillingness to accept that tragedy can be exist without needing to be meant.

This is usually where someone reaches for "Well, it's all a mystery."

But saying that already assumes there's a "why." It's staring at the mountain and inventing reasons for its existence rather than asking *how* it came to be. And "how" is the only question that leads us anywhere useful.

This is why that mindset isn't just unhelpful: it's harmful. "Why" distracts us from solutions.

"How" shifts the problem into the realm of science, not metaphysics. We can study, test, and understand. We can uncover mechanisms, identify causes, and work toward prevention or eradication. We can treat leukemia not as a divine message, but as a biological flaw to be solved.

That is helpful. That is progress. Shrugging our shoulders at a "mystery" is not. We don't need to preserve the illusion that a hidden purpose makes suffering acceptable. We don't need to bow to some invisible parent in the sky. We need to roll up our sleeves and make sure no child has to endure it again.

Some might suggest you can do both; we can ask 'how' while still holding to religious beliefs. In practice, that's true. There are religious scientists who tirelessly work on cures, who embody compassion and rigor. They are good people. But even then, the "mystery" mindset quietly shapes the limits of inquiry. It might not directly guide the hand of those scientists, but it certainly influences where those hands work.

If you believe suffering is ultimately part of a divine plan, you've already conceded that it is *meant* to happen. And that believe can blunt the urgency to eliminate it. Because if that suffering is necessary, then eradicating it would be working against God's will.

Of course, I don't think rational humans consciously think that way. But that idea still lurks in the background, influencing where research, money, and policy go. It invites complacency or indifference where there should be relentless defiance.

In 2025, we've already seen government funding cuts for critical medical and scientific initiatives. This comes at a time when we've seen a resurgence in religious belief across the country, and a rise in religious rhetoric from our politicians. Do I believe these politicians *want* more childhood cancer? Of course not.

But I do believe that a worldview which treats suffering as divinely ordained makes those cuts easier to tolerate. It turns a solvable problem into a sacred inevitability. And once you call something inevitable, once you frame it as part of a plan, you stop fighting it with the urgency it deserves. You put the beaker down and hold your hands to pray the cancer away instead.

I experienced this first hand in hospital rooms and at our front door. Doctors told us of parents who refused cancer treatment for their children on religious grounds. Religious groups who stood on our porch warning us of the divine perils of blood transfusions. One woman told me there are "other options" and "different futures" for Ellie - presumably a noble death - instead of life saving blood transfusions. If I allowed another person's blood into her body, I would be replacing Ellie's soul with someone else's. God wouldn't like that. By "save her," they presumably meant the type of salvation that comes after her death.

I used to think most people didn't *really* believe the religious nonsense they repeated. But for many, when their child was truly suffering and *could* be spared, they chose superstitions over their kin. And from their perspective, why wouldn't they? They were abiding by the will of their

146

creator. In their eyes, they were not doing harm. Quite the opposite: they were fulfilling God's plan. That child, they believed, would live on in the afterlife, anyway.

That's the not-so-quiet cost of the "it's all a mystery" mindset. It plants the seed that "this is the way things are meant to be." That seed is watered by every shrug, every prayer in place of action, and every rationalization that "God knows best." It grows like a weed, twisting and trapping everything in its path, choking out healthier harvest.

Meanwhile, real children in real hospital beds wait for answers we already have tools to find. Or in some cases, answers we already have. They wait for treatments that exist but are withheld. They wait for cures that could come sooner. They wait while billions nod along, mistaking fatalism for faith.

The "mystery" isn't *why* they're sick. The mystery is why, in a world with the knowledge, resources, and skill to do better, we cling to ancient superstitions to dictate whether a child lives or dies. The truth is, it isn't a mystery at all. It's a choice. A choice reinforced with every "God has a plan" or "this is happening for a reason."

When confronted with these platitudes, my responses were usually restrained. I genuinely believe most people who say these things mean well. Religion has monopolized morality so completely that phrases like "God has a plan" are reflexively seen as kind, even virtuous. For many, the idea that they might be saying something harmful never even crosses their mind. So how should we respond?

At first, I defaulted to politeness. I'd nod, change the subject, or offer something vague and noncommittal. When someone offered to pray for Ellie, I'd quietly say "thank you" and move on. More than once, someone offered to connect me with religious support groups that could help me with the "why" questions I must be facing. I'd smile and reply, "I'm okay, thank you."

I told myself this was out of respect. That dismantling someone's worldview wouldn't help Ellie. That arguing over theology wasn't worth the emotional bandwidth.

But over time, I began to wonder if my politeness was really just cowardice in disguise. By staying quiet, I was letting harmful ideas pass unchallenged. I was allowing well-meaning but corrosive notions to keep circulating unchecked. Every time I nodded politely, I was helping ensure those same platitudes would be passed on to the next parent, and the one after that.

Some ideas deserve a more direct answer. English actor, writer, and outspoken atheist Stephen Fry once gave one of most unflinching answers I've ever heard when asked what he would say to God if they met.

> *"I'd say 'bone cancer in children?' What's that about? How dare you? How dare you create a world in which there's such misery that's not our fault. It's not right. It's utterly, utterly, evil. Why should I respect a capricious, mean-minded, stupid God who creates a world that is so full of injustice and pain? Yes, the world is very splendid, but it also has in it insects whose whole life cycle is to borrow in the eyes of children and make them blind. It eats outwards from the eyes. Why? Why did it do that? You could have made a creation in which that didn't exist. It is simply unacceptable."*

148

Fry's words echoed in me, giving voice to every ounce of frustration I'd tried to rationalize. They changed how I showed up in conversations with family, friends, or even strangers. I began to feel a responsibility to speak more honestly on the topic. It wasn't about attacking beliefs or shaming anyone. It was a resistance to the normalization of ideas that excuse suffering.

When someone offered "prayers" or spoke of "a reason" as a shield against the harsh reality Ellie faced, I learned to respond differently. It wasn't easy. It meant risking awkwardness, challenging deeply held convictions, and sometimes feeling isolated. But I realized that silence was its own kind of complicity.

Now, when offered prayers, I say "I appreciate the gesture and hope prayer brings you peace. We're placing our faith in doctors and modern medicine instead."

When someone mentioned God's plan for Ellie, I'd reply, "I don't think there's any plan that justifies a three year old getting cancer."

Some might hear this and think I'm being confrontational or inconsiderate. That's not my intention. My goal isn't to criticize or shame anyone's beliefs; it's to invite honesty. I want to foster genuine dialogue, encourage deeper reflection, and challenge unhelpful assumptions. I want conversations that confront difficult truths and help us think differently about suffering and hope. And, in my experience, these kinds of exchanges often lead to something powerful and productive.

Over of the most helpful set of conversations I had during Ellie's treatment was with a deeply religious friend.

He's a devout Christian who takes his faith seriously, but he's also curious, thoughtful, and deeply respectful of others' beliefs. Shortly after Ellie's diagnosis, he called and offered something beautifully different.

"Louie," he said, "You know I'm going to pray for Ellie. But I know that's not your thing and I respect that. So I want to support you in some other way that might help. Cancer isn't the only thing going on in your life. I'd love to call you and talk about whatever else is on your mind when you want to chat. Does that work for you?"

It was such a simple gesture, yet it meant everything. We began talking every other week for an hour. We spoke about home projects, music, and our fitness goals. The hour often stretched longer, yet it always felt too short. That block of time on my calendar became an oasis of normalcy. During those calls, I wasn't a cancer parent. I was just a friend talking to another friend about whatever friends talk about. Occasionally, I'd mention a hospital story or a sleepless night, but it was never the focus. For that short time, I wasn't thinking about lab results or chemotherapy schedules. I just got to be me.

I'll remember those conversations for the rest of my life. What may have been a simple act from a friend resulted a monumental shift in my mental wellbeing.

Other moments of normalcy helped too - poker nights with the neighbors, laughing about terrible hands; swapping weekend soccer highlights with friends who knew I might have spent the day at the clinic; or the friends who treated Ellie like any other four year old kid. I didn't always want to talk about leukemia. Those moments reminded me that I didn't have to.

That is what helped us endure. They were the building blocks of a life that felt, somehow, whole again.

But what worked for us might not make sense for everyone else. We're all different. There is no one size fits all approach to talking to a someone facing this sort of hardship. Often, a simple conversation about *how* to help is the best place to start.

Even a few honest words like "I'm here for you" or "This is awful, it must feel so unfair" can make a difference. They don't pretend the world makes sense. They don't strip someone of agency and point toward a deity at work. They acknowledge pain for what it is, and they offer real empathy. Sometimes, that's all that's needed: an open door, an invitation to talk, a willingness to sit in the discomfort together.

Because conversation is what pushes progress forward, both personally and collectively.

We cannot accept iron-aged superstitions about metaphysical purpose when children suffer in cancer clinics. We must demand better of ourselves and of our leaders. We must stop gazing up at the sky and asking 'why' and instead look down into microscopes and ask 'how.'

How can we ensure no child ever faces what Ellie endured? How can we fund science and health initiatives that eradicate cancer once and for all? How can we continuously march toward reducing suffering in the world?

And the ultimate 'how' question that drives all of human behavior: how can we make our lives better tomorrow than it was today?

Seeking answers to those questions doesn't require a plan. It requires showing up, choosing action over complacency, and not settling for comforting answers when deeper truths are to be found.

That's not divine. That's human. And I'll take that every time.

12
Charleston

A different kind of faith began to take shape in the spring of 2024. Not the kind I'd wrestled in late-night conversations about God, but one built from smaller, sturdier pieces. We had started opening our lives again, no longer confining ourselves to hospital rooms and clinic visits. We said yes to play dates and birthday parties. We brought Ellie and Rosie to morning story time at the local library and spent afternoons at the park. The more we let the outside world in, the more normal things began to feel.

It was a quiet, deliberate faith in Ellie's treatment plan that propelled us forward. The medicine was working. The routines we had built with such care were holding, giving shape and steadiness to our days. Fragility and fear never fully disappeared, but they were slowly being edged out by an optimism we hadn't felt in over a year.

In 2023, we had lived one day at a time, hoping only to reach tomorrow. Now, for the first time, we had reason to plan ahead. Ellie's lab results continued to improve with each visit. Surgical procedures appeared on the calendar less often, and medication reminders became slightly less frequent. Leukemia was still a massive presence in our lives, but we could picture a day when it might not be.

Ellie had grown up so much, too. She wasn't the baby or toddler I still sometimes pictured her as. She was a kid. At four and a half, she was writing her own name across hand-drawn drawings and singing to herself in the shower. She didn't ask for a push on the swing-set anymore and grabbed her own snacks from the pantry when she was hungry. The meandering, whimsical chatter of a toddler had given way to real conversations I genuinely looked forward to. Watching her, I realized she was no longer defined by the months of hospitals and medicine, but by the little person she was becoming.

Fifteen months ago, I wasn't sure we'd get here. I can still see that hotel room, still hear Emily saying the word *cancer*, still feel the world spinning beneath me. I can still hear the thump of the music from the room next door, a strange reminder that life outside our own had gone on. That following morning, I woke up struggling to grasp the weight of it all. I might have told myself Ellie would make it through this, but I'm not sure I ever fully believed it at the time.

Those nightmarish memories will never leave me, but I'm not sure I want them to. They're painful, but they keep me grateful. Like the Stoics, I'm reminded of what could have been, and how fortunate we are that those alternative realities didn't come to pass. The past fifteen months were unchangeable. The only question left was the same as it always had been: *That happened. Now what?*

This time, the answer felt lighter. The "now what" wasn't about survival; it was about who Ellie gets to become. The future finally seemed brighter, filled with firsts our family had been waiting so long for.

It began with preschool paperwork. I nearly dried out the yellow highlighter as I combed through each orientation packet line by line. I dove headfirst into research about preschool curricula, read reviews from other parents, dissected school ratings, and scrutinized safety measures. I built pro-and-con lists like my daughter's future depended on it. Because it did. Emily and I spent hours talking about which preschool would give Ellie the best start. Eventually, we chose one just minutes from home and scheduled a tour for the following week.

The morning of the tour began, in some ways, like any other. My routine was automatic now: wake up at 5:00 a.m., read, work out, shower, and sip coffee before the house stirred. The same steady habits that carried me through the hardest season were now carrying me into a better one. Every routine felt like a quiet promise I was keeping to myself, and to Ellie, that we were ready for what came next. Only this time, it wasn't about enduring. It was about thriving.

As I finished my coffee at the kitchen table, I couldn't ignore the contrast. Fifteen months ago, I'd been in this same seat, in a house just as quiet, but the table told a different story. Back then, it was covered in printouts about chemotherapy side effects, fever protocols, and emergency contact lists. Now, it was stacked with preschool packets and crayon-colored calendars. My routines once served as a

155

lifeline, keeping me afloat. Now, those same routines were tools for building a better life.

The framework that once kept me grounded during sleepless nights and endless hospital visits had transformed. In those early days, when everything felt out control, focusing on each moment was the only way forward. It wasn't just about surviving. It was about choosing what to hold onto and how to find meaning in the smallest victories. Now, as I prepared for Ellie's first day of preschool, that same mindset guided me. Except this time, hope replaced fear. What was once a means of enduring hardship was now a path to embracing life.

Maximizing each moment took on a different form. Soon, our family would embark on new beginnings, make new memories, and reach new milestones. How could I show up in those moments to make the most out of each one? It was the same question I had always asked myself, but now, it carried the lightness of optimism.

I scrolled through photo albums of Ellie on my phone. Months earlier, those pictures had been painful to look at. I'd see her full head of curly red hair and her wide smile and ache for easier times. I'd look at photos from the weeks before her diagnosis and wonder how we missed it. Her skin had grown paler with each image, her eyes more tired just days before the phone call that confirmed our worst fears. For months, I tortured myself with questions that had no answers. Could I have helped her sooner? Could I have done something differently? Those late-night hypotheticals never helped anyone. They only kept me trapped in a past I couldn't change.

But I didn't ask those questions anymore.

Now, I just saw Ellie. I saw a sweet little girl who brought joy to everyone she met. A kid who endured something no child should ever and did so with a grit and grace I'll never match. I saw her for who she was. Not as she'd been before leukemia, not through the lens of fear or regret, but exactly as she was now. A child with a limitless future ahead of her. And today, that future was just beginning.

Maximizing each moment meant being fully here without the weight of yesterday's regrets or the haze of tomorrow's what-ifs. It meant showing up, seeing clearly, and allowing joy to exist right alongside uncertainty.

Ellie tiptoed down the steps quietly and smiled when she saw me at the table. "Daddy, can we read books together?"

It was a routine we reserved for special mornings. Whenever she woke up early, Ellie would make her way downstairs, careful not to wake the rest of the house. We'd curl up on the couch and read together in the stillness of the day.

She wrapped her arms around me tightly on the couch and looked up. "I'm nervous about preschool."

"It's okay to be nervous, Ellie," I began, "I get nervous about a lot of things!"

"Even grown ups get nervous?" she asked.

I put my arm around her, the way she had done with me so many times. Her hair was starting to grow back, faint wisps of curls catching the morning light. "Of course we do! Everyone gets nervous. But I bet you're also pretty excited, right?"

"Yeah," she smirked, "I can't wait to see the playground."

"When I feel nervous, I try think about the fun things I'll get to do. Maybe you'll meet a new friend or go down a super fast slide or play with new toys. Sometimes talking about the exciting parts makes the nervous parts feel smaller."

She nodded. "I'm still nervous, but I am really excited to go down the slide at the playground."

"I'm really excited for you to do that too," I said, smiling.

She leaned into me, and it was clear that we were both still learning the same lesson. You don't have to wait for the fear to disappear before you let yourself feel joy. There would be plenty of unknowns in the year ahead: new germs she might catch, new bumps and bruises, new classmates who wouldn't understand why she had to leave early for doctor's appointments.

But right now, all that could wait. Ellie's soft hair brushed against my cheek, the morning light streamed through the window, and there was the promise of a slide she couldn't wait to go down. I felt completely content to just be here, in this moment.

The preschool tour couldn't have gone better. Ellie beamed at her classroom, explored the giant playground, sat in on a gymnastics class, and met her teachers. She walked the colorful hallways like she already belonged there. The next morning, she asked how many days were left until school started.

We signed the paperwork the next afternoon. In the fall, Ellie would be a preschooler.

We still had the whole summer ahead of us. There were months to fill with new adventures, small rituals, and the kind of days that stretch lazily from sunrise to sunset. We had time to open ourselves up, say yes to more, and see where each day might lead.

We decided to start the summer with a trip to Charleston, South Carolina. Only three hours away, it was far enough to feel like a vacation, but close enough to make it back quickly if Ellie got sick. Charleston felt like the right mix of charm and adventure - colorful houses, cobblestone streets, and salty air drifting in from the ocean.

For Ellie and Rosie, it wasn't about the history or the architecture. Their joy would come from the little things, like seeing palm trees for the first time or visiting the ice cream shop where they piled on whatever toppings they wanted. Some days we spent hours at the beach digging holes so big the girls could sit inside them, only to watch the tide fill them back in. Other days we let the city lead us, wandering down alleys and across city squares without an agenda.

It was a significant shift for Emily and me. For over a year, saying "no" to adventures had become second nature. From declining playdates to avoiding public places, "no" had become our default. Mostly, it was justified: we had to keep Ellie safe. Seeing other people or visiting new places often meant exposure to germs, and for so long, "getting sick" would have been catastrophic.

But holding on that tightly had its own cost. We were learning that safety could keep Ellie alive, but it couldn't make her feel alive. At some point, protecting her from every risk meant robbing her of every joy. It's hard to live in the moment when there are no moments to live in.

We could see the restlessness building in both Ellie and Rosie. They weren't worried about germs or setbacks. They just wanted to play, explore, and be kids.

Charleston gave us permission to loosen our grip. For once, our days weren't dictated by treatments or schedules. Lab results showed Ellie's immune system slowly recovering, too. If there was ever a time to change our default "no" to a "yes," this trip was it. And that's exactly what we did.

One afternoon we passed a courtyard where kids were splashing in a fountain. Ellie froze, eyes wide, watching the water shoot up twice her height. Before I could say anything, she looked at me and asked, "Can I?"

A year earlier, the answer would have been obvious. Absolutely not. Too many kids, too many germs, too many ways things could go wrong. But that afternoon. Emily and I traded a look and instead of no, we said yes.

Shoes came off. Giggles turned into shrieks of joy. Within seconds, Ellie was off chasing the streams, soaked from head to toe. For that moment, there wasn't a single care in the world.

That day was a turning point in how we thought about Ellie's remaining treatment. For fifteen months, we hadn't had the autonomy to make many parenting decisions. Our lives were on autopilot, guided by chemotherapy schedules and side effects. We wanted to say "yes" more often, but we couldn't. We accepted that. We were willing to make any sacrifice to keep Ellie safe.

But Charleston reminded us that Ellie wasn't at the beginning of her treatment anymore. We didn't have to live in lockdown. The world was ready to open up again if we were willing to open up with it. We could still keep Ellie safe while helping her rediscover a childhood worth remembering.

So we did just that.

We stayed up too late, slept in too long, and ate pancakes at the corner diner before deciding what to do next. Charleston was the kind of place where saying yes felt natural. Ellie and Rosie felt it, too. We could see it in the sparkle of their eyes, in the way their laughter lingered long after we'd said goodnight. They sensed it as clearly as we did: life didn't have to be full of "no" anymore.

It was June of 2024. Ellie still had eight months of treatment left, and we didn't fool ourselves into thinking leukemia was behind us. But we didn't linger on it, either. It would have been easy to hold back and wait for a safer time when life felt more predictable. But the girls weren't waiting. They craved normalcy more than we did. Watching them roll in the sand and splash barefoot through fountains reminded us that normalcy wouldn't simply arrive on its own. We had to create it.

By the time we packed up the car to head home, it wasn't just a trip we were bringing back. It was a reminder that the present moment is always enough.

We carried that spirit into the rest of the summer. Some nights, we let the girls stay up late, curled on the couch with movies and takeout pizza. Others days we spent entirely outside blowing bubbles, lounging at the community pool, or passing the soccer ball around until he sun went down. We didn't need cobblestone streets or palm trees. Charleston had taught us was that letting go wasn't just for vacation. We could make the most out of each moment right where we were, even with the cancer treatment schedule still taped to our refrigerator.

13
Growing

The summer of 2024 marked a turning point. Hope was outrunning hardship, shaping both Ellie's treatment and the rhythm of our daily lives. The weight of a leukemia diagnosis didn't disappear, but our strength to carry it had grown. That strength was forged in a mental framework tested on the hardest of days.

But life has a way of checking whether the lessons you've claimed to learn have actually taken root, and that summer was no exception.

It was a season that tested everything I thought I'd learned about handling life's uncertainty. My Grandpa on my Mom's side passed away that summer. Though he was nearly 90 when he left us, his death felt unexpected. It wasn't death itself that was surprised us, but the sudden absence of his presence. Grandpa was one of those people you simply assumed would *always* be there. And then one day, he wasn't.

Born in Italy in 1935, he left for America in 1967 in pursuit of the American dream. He opened a successful food business soon after arriving and never looked back. Grandpa brought love and laughter to everything he touched, and his presence always felt steady and reassuring.

Nothing made him happier than surrounding himself with family. Nearly every Sunday of my childhood was spent around a dinner table with Grandpa at the center. He was the most boisterous, hilarious person I've ever met and I looked forward to seeing him every weekend. His stories could fill a night and leave everyone doubled over with laughter. After dinner, we'd watch soccer and play card games late into the evening.

As I grew older, we only grew closer. In college, I'd invite him to play poker with my friends. After the weekend soccer games, he'd call me to debate which teams had a real shot at the title. Even after Ellie's diagnosis, he'd call to check on her, always asking how he could help.

Toward the end of his life, he never lost an ounce of what made him so loved. The last time we spoke, he was teasing me about the time he had four-of-a-kind and knocked me out of a poker tournament. He was still sharing stories with hospital staff too, making sure no one left his room without a smile. The nurses told us he was their favorite patient. That surprised no one.

Grandpa lived an incredible life. At 89, he had three kids, six grandchildren, and seven great grandchildren. We'll always be grateful for the opportunities he created and the example he set. His life was defined by generosity, determination, and devotion to family. I learned so much from the path he paved.

But even as we celebrated the fullness of his life, I felt the familiar curiosity of how to process death itself.

When Nonno passed away, my head had been filled with 'why' questions. At 17, I couldn't make sense of death. I grasped for answers that weren't there, searched for meaning where none could be found.

Now 35, Grandpa's death was an entirely different experience. I didn't waste time asking 'why.' The framework I honed during Ellie's treatment trained me to look for the 'how,' instead. And that's exactly what I did.

Rather than getting lost in grief or searching for meaning that wasn't there, I focused on how I could honor Grandpa's legacy in everyday moments. I leaned into the family around me, held my daughters a little tighter, and reminded myself to be present with them. We cooked breakfast together while I shared stories about working the cash register on Grandpa's food truck. We giggled at pictures of Grandpa's toothless grin and the funny faces he used to make. I told them about his journey from Italy to America and how brave he was. I only wish they'd had more time to know him.

Focusing on 'how' rather than 'why' allowed me to actually process death and move forward. I wasn't trapped in a fog, demanding answers I'd never get. I didn't dwell on the unfairness of his final days, like I did with Nonno. I didn't pray for clarity or search for some hidden plan. Instead, I made the conscious choice to celebrate the life Grandpa lived. That choice made room for presence in this moment. It was quiet and somber, but calm.

That doesn't mean grief didn't come. It did, in waves. Focusing on the 'how' didn't erase the injustice that life must end: it reframed it. It reminded me that the brevity of life doesn't diminish its meaning. It only amplifies the moments we do have.

The fleeting nature of life fuels the need for presence. To pin hope on an afterlife or posthumous reunion with loved ones risks diluting the now. It suggests there will always be more time, more chances. But there aren't. When we understand that present is all we truly possess, its value expands. Every laugh at the dinner table, every story shared, every tiny hug before bedtime becomes enough. Because it is all there is.

If life is finite, then each moment isn't ordinary: it's irreplaceable. And that truth changes how we move through the world.

Ellie's diagnosis forced that lesson into reality. Presence wasn't optional. I didn't know if there would be a "tomorrow." I couldn't live in some imagined future where treatment was behind us, nor could I afford to replay the terror of her diagnosis on repeat. Both robbed me of what I actually had: Ellie, here, now. Sitting beside her on a hospital bed, watching her sleep, coloring together, or laughing at her silly jokes weren't just ways to pass the time. They were the entire point. They were life.

Grandpa's death put that lesson into perspective on a larger scale. It took the fragments of everything I'd been learning and assembled them into something I could actually hold onto. It was his one final gift, his last lesson before he passed.

I thought of that when, at Grandpa's funeral, Ellie tugged at my sleeve.

"What does dead mean? What's going to happen to your Grandpa?" she asked.

She wasn't even five. It was the first time we'd brushed against anything resembling philosophy or metaphysics, though wrapped in preschool language.

"Well," I said carefully, "no one really knows what happens when people die. Everyone believes something different."

She tilted her head, wanting more. "Do we get to see him after today?"

"I don't think we will, Ellie. When people die, their bodies stop working. But that doesn't mean we forget about them. We can always remember Grandpa's stories or the silly things he did. That way, part of him stays with us forever."

She smiled. "Yeah, he was funny."

That was all she needed, for now. She didn't have to make sense of death or understand the fragility of life. One day, Ellie and Rosie may take her own journeys through the 'why' questions I did, but it wasn't going to be today.

As a parent, my wish is to raise children who are curious, freethinking, and unshackled by dogma. It wasn't my place to hand them answers or persuade their thinking. My role is to protect their freedom to ask questions and to discover whatever truths they seek.

Raising children isn't about shielding them from every challenge. It's about arming them with a toolkit for life's inevitable twists and turns. I hope Ellie and Rosie learn that their toolkits are never complete. There's always a learning opportunity around the bend that will help sharpen a tool they didn't know they needed.

The past year or two had plenty of winding roads for our family to navigate. Early on, the bumps felt unbearable. But now, as life's challenges still came barreling toward us, they felt more like speed bumps. They might have temporarily slowed us down, but they wouldn't stop us.

It was this mindset, fueled by the framework I was consistently strengthening, that helped us get through the final days of summer.

Those lessons in presence, honed through grief, became a lifeline just weeks later when Ellie fell ill.

In the past, the first sign of Ellie being sick would send me spiraling ahead, imagining every terrible possibility. I had taken the Stoic practice of *premeditatio malorum* far beyond its intent. In the past, I wasn't preparing for hardship; I was living inside it. Over time, I refined that approach.

My reaction to life's difficulties was shifting. I was measured, calm, and in control. The fear was still there, but it didn't run the show.

So when Ellie spiked a fever on a Sunday night, my immediate thoughts weren't panic-driven. They were rational and measured, like a script I'd rehearsed to stay steady when life veered off course. The framework I'd been practicing all year wasn't about eliminating fear, but about knowing where to place it.

Early in Ellie's diagnosis, I would have walked into the emergency room asking, *why us? Why does this keep happening? What if this never ends?*

But now, I only thought, *what is in front of me right now? What step can I take next?* That shift changed everything. I was in the moment.

Stoicism taught me that fear is a story I tell myself, not an inevitability or a sign of things to come. I couldn't answer why she was sick, but I could focus on how to help her through it. How to hold her hand during the swabs. How to make her laugh in a room full of machines.

After hours of being poked and prodded and being awakened to check vitals throughout the night, Ellie was diagnosed with Covid. There is no philosophical blueprint or mindful meditation that will strip the pain away from seeing your child in pain. Nothing can ease the hurt in your heart when you know they're suffering.

But with a mind cleared of 'why' questions, I was free to focus on the 'how.' I couldn't cure her illness; that was out of my hands. But I could put all my energy behind how to hold her hand through the nasal swabs, how to make her smile when she was scared, how help her laugh in a room that felt so heavy. In doing so, I was firmly in the moment.

What struck me most wasn't my own shift, but Ellie's. The first time we came to the emergency room, she was terrified, clinging to me and asking endless questions about what would come next. This time, she entire attitude had changed. She still winced at the needles, but she held her hand out bravely. She still looked to me, but more to see if I was smiling than if I was scared. The effects of the virus were still painful, but her ability to endure them grew beyond our imagination. Her bravery and resilience are things I still marvel at.

Her body was recovering, too. Lab results indicated that she would be able to recovery from the illness all on her own, without intervention. Instead of a week-long stay, we were discharged the following morning.

For us, this was no small victory. It was the first time in years the path ahead felt shorter than the road behind. Normally, we left the hospital only after rounds of transfusions and endless IV medications. This time, we left with nothing but discharge paperwork.

The lab results hinted she was getting better, but Ellie made it undeniable the next morning. When we carefully opened her bedroom door, we braced for a tired little girl still recovering from a late night in the ER.

Instead, we found her wide awake, twirling and singing. She had lined up all of her stuffed animals on her bed and was serenading them with her own made up songs.

She paused when the door opened. "You're late for the concert," she said, her eyes bright. "Come on in."

It would have been easy to mistake that moment as ordinary. A little girl singing to her stuffed animals. But for us, it wasn't ordinary at all. Ordinary had been stolen from us long ago, but this was its silhouette returning.

Watching her sing, it was clear that Ellie was living the lesson I had been trying to learn: joy isn't found after suffering ends, but in the spaces where we allow it to return. The sound of her laughter filled more than just her room that morning. It spilled into the rest of us too, loosening something that had been tight in our chests for months.

It was progress. Not imagined. Not hoped for. It was real. Lab results and discharge paperwork were great, of course. But what mattered most was here, in this room: Ellie, happy again.

Ellie's resilience and joy reminded me how rare and precious these moments were. I was also overwhelmed with appreciation for the people that made it possible. There were doctors and nurses we met, researchers and donors we hadn't. There were volunteers who worked tirelessly behind the scenes to make the world safer and brighter for kids like

Ellie. And there were family and friends who offered support that went above and beyond what we could ever ask for.

Every act of care, every small kindness, added up to something larger than ourselves. It was a network of grace that allowed us to breathe, to smile, and to witness her laughter that morning. It wasn't a miracle or a blessing; it was the result of countless hands and hearts working together to make life a bit easier for a little girl and her family.

In the past, I hadn't known how to carry that kind of generosity. Guilt often crept in, whispering that we were taking more than we deserved. But not here. Not now. As Ellie sang the final song of her stuffed animal concert, I only felt gratitude. It was an overwhelming thankfulness for the simple gift of being present in this moment.

Emily felt it, too. That night, we talked about how different our lives had been a year earlier, and how different they might be in a year from now. We reflected on how fortunate we were, how thankful we felt for the love and support that had carried Ellie forward. We decided that, if ever given the chance, we wanted to make a difference in the lives of other children. It wasn't about evening the scales or paying off some imagined debt. It was simply the right thing to do.

We couldn't promise that every child's story would unfold like Ellie's, but we could promise moments - brief flashes of joy, however small, for families like ours. Emily scribbled *Strong Like Ellie Foundation* in the margins of a notebook, and we agreed to revisit it after Ellie rang the bell.

We closed the notebook that night with a promise to save the dream for a later day. But before we could even imagine making a difference for other families, an organization appeared to make a difference for ours: Make-A-Wish.

I had known of Make-A-Wish long before Ellie's diagnosis. Years earlier, I volunteered with the organization, helping grant wishes to other children. Through a company I worked for at the time, I'd also supported fundraising for the foundation. I vividly remember handing over oversized checks, watching videos of families learning their child's wish. I remember the sparkle in their eyes, the way a trip or an experience could lift a whole family out of the heaviness of illness, if only for a moment. Back then, I saw it from the outside. I never truly understood the depth of what it meant.

When I first heard Ellie would be eligible for that same gift, I wasn't sure how to feel. Part of me recoiled, as if accepting something so generous meant admitting how serious her illness really was. Another part of me wrestled with guilt: Ellie *would* recover, but other children wouldn't. Shouldn't they get their wish granted first? It was the same tension that had followed me all along, the uneasy balance between grace and guilt.

Grace wanted me to simply receive, but guilt whispered that we were taking too much. In those early conversations, I wasn't sure which voice to believe.

But now, more than a year since our first conversation with Make-A-Wish, it became real. In the spring of 2025, our family would be given the gift of a week-long stay in Disney World in Orlando, Florida. It was an all expenses paid trip that included passes to every park, front of the line access to every ride, and just about every bell and whistle imaginable.

As the details unfolded, I began to see this gift differently. This wasn't charity, nor was handed down out of pity. It was grace, woven through the generosity of countless strangers who wanted to give families like ours something medicine couldn't offer: joyful memories of time spent together.

Like the Charlotte supporters proudly wearing the scarves Ellie designed, this wasn't an act of obligation, it was an act of love. It was recognition that Ellie was seen, celebrated, and never alone. It was an acknowledgement of the many days Ellie had endured what no child should ever face. More than anything, it was an opportunity to put that world behind us for seven days in the happiest place on Earth.

A year ago, I would have lost sleep over the guilt of accepting a gift so generous. But that guilt was replaced by an overwhelming gratitude for the kindness of strangers.

In the end, I realized this is what it means to be human. We hold one another up in the hardest moments, bringing joy into spaces that should only hold sorrow. Life isn't a ledger, and love isn't an exchange. We don't keep score. We give, we lift, and we carry. And when our turn comes, the only task is to receive with open hands. It isn't charity; it's connection.

Our responsibility and our promise was to help Ellie and Rosie understand that lesson. When we told them about Disney, we made sure to explain not just where we were going, but how this gift came to be and who made it possible. We wanted them to see that this wasn't just about a vacation; it was about the kindness and care of strangers. We shared stories of people donating their time, energy, and resources to honor Ellie's journey.

We wanted them to understand that every ride, every parade, every laugh that waited for us in Orlando was built on the compassion of people who would never meet us, yet still chose to care. That kind of generosity has its own quiet magic, the kind that reaches farther than any magic wand could.

We also marked it on our calendar as the celebration of an incredibly special day. Just a few weeks before our trip to Disney, Ellie would ring the bell. By the time we stepped into the Magic Castle, she would no longer be a leukemia patient. She would be a survivor.

14
Moving Forward

On a brisk September morning, I walked into the kitchen to find Emily carefully brushing Ellie's hair. Her reddish-brown curls tumbled over her ears, wild and untamed, like Annie in her prime. Ellie's hair hadn't fully returned to its pre-chemotherapy length yet, but it was well on its way. Looking at her now, it seemed impossible that her head was once bare at all. Mornings like this felt like they were borrowed from another life, as if the last year was a nightmare I'd just woken from. Emily clipped in a small, pink bow while Ellie talked a mile a minute about her upcoming first day of school.

What struck me more than her hair, though, was her energy. It buzzed through the room the way light fills a window, bright and impossible to ignore. She was already telling Rosie about the school playground and all the friends she was sure to meet there.

For months, we carried Ellie through treatment, coaxing her to eat, urging her to walk, and watching her drift in and out of exhaustion. Now, she was carrying us. She was the life and soul of our home. She reminded us in the simplest, loudest ways that joy wasn't something fragile to be tiptoed around, but something to be lived in fully. I remember her standing there in the kitchen, bow in her hair, looking every bit like a preschooler ready to take on the world.

This is what healing actually looked like. It wasn't the absence of sickness; it was the unstoppable return of spirit. Not some metaphysical, untouchable spirit, but the kind we could hear in her voice, see in her smile, and feel in the strength of her morning hug.

In a past life, I would've worried about her first day of school. Would she catch a cold from another kid in class? Would her leukemia come up in conversation? What if someone bumped into her port on the playground? Do we need to pull her out for treatment? My mind used to live in these spirals, scanning every possible threat, as if enough vigilance could protect her from the chaos of life.

Now, I see things differently. Fear hasn't disappeared, but it no longer runs the show. My framework, grounded in a kind of everyday stoicism, has shifted. I can't control whether Ellie gets a runny nose, or whether another child asks an awkward question, or whether life blindsides us again with something we never saw coming. What I can control is my response. I can show up steady. I can focus on what's in front of me, not the thousand imagined futures that may never arrive.

Preparing for the randomness of the universe is a fool's errand. Life has already proven to me, in ways I never asked for, that no amount of planning can bend the world into predictability. I can memorize hospital protocols, lay out my clothes the night before, and line backpacks by the garage door, but the truth is that most of what matters sits well beyond my grasp.

That doesn't mean planning is useless. Preparation has its place. Over the past year, the only order we've known lived in the routines we created. But there's a line I used to cross, where planning slipped into control-seeking, as if I could outsmart uncertainty itself. That kind of living is a slow suffocation, because it ties your peace to outcomes that don't belong to you.

What I'm learning instead is to prepare lightly, and then release. To accept that life is built on chance and circumstance as much as it is on discipline. When I hold too tightly, I break. When I let go, I bend. That's the paradox the Stoics understood so well: strength isn't in resistance, it's in alignment. It's not about hardening against the world, but learning to move with it. Resilience isn't found in trying to prevent every storm. It's found in knowing you can walk through the storm when it comes.

So on a morning like this, we can pack her lunch, we can make sure her hair is neatly brushed, and we can check the seatbelt twice on the drive to school. But the rest is for the universe to decide. My role is to be steady and grounded enough to meet whatever happens with clarity and reason.

Ellie taught me this more than any philosophy book could. Hearing her laugh on mornings when she had energy, or watching her dance around the living room on a Wednesday night after chemotherapy, Ellie showed me that life doesn't wait for perfect conditions. It's lived right here, with whatever hand you've been dealt. That realization didn't just change how I look at her first day of school: it changed how I look at every single moment, cutting through the illusion that control is a prerequisite for joy.

Still, the moments of this morning will stay etched into me forever. Every parent remembers their child's first day of school. But not many parents spend sleepless nights wondering if their child will ever get one. The ordinary becomes sacred when you've lived through its absence. Packing a lunchbox. Zipping a backpack. Watching her shoes dangle from the car seat. These small moments, forgettable to most, were proof that life had returned to us, piece by fragile piece.

The day had finally arrived: not as a miracle to be explained, but as life itself, moving forward.

I grabbed her hand as we walked to the car, her grip tiny but certain. For so long, I had imagined this day with hesitation, with fear of what could go wrong. But standing there in the driveway, watching her climb into the backseat, all I felt was the sheer, unshakable gratitude of watching her go. I didn't just see Ellie going to her first day of school: I saw Ellie heading toward everything that was waiting for her in life.

When we pulled into the school parking lot, I caught myself scanning every detail. There were oversized backpacks bouncing on little shoulders, teachers waving at the curb, and emotional parents savoring each moment. It was exactly what I could expect on the first day of preschool. That's what struck me the most. This moment that once seemed like a distant hope was playing out with the same simplicity as it did for everyone else.

Ellie's teacher came to our car to hold Ellie's hand and walk her into the school. Ellie anxiously walked toward the entrance, looking back over her shoulder just once before slipping through the double doors that marked the start of something entirely new.

The road ahead was still lined with chemotherapy appointments, procedures, and lab results. But today wasn't about what lay ahead for Ellie. Today, she was just a little girl walking into her first day of school. And for the first time in a long time, that was enough. I didn't need to see beyond those double doors. It was enough to know that she'd walked through them.

Back home, I kept glancing at the clock not out of worry, but out of excitement. Each hour felt full of possibility, wondering how Ellie's day was unfolding.

I imagined her laughter spilling into the classroom, the way it did at home during our pretend tea parties. I pictured her raising her hand to answer a question, or introducing herself to new friends. More than anything, I was excited for everyone to meet this incredible girl that had changed our lives.

By the time the school day ended, my excitement had turned into a quiet, steady gratitude. When Emily walked back through the door, Ellie trailed quickly behind, cheeks flush from running and laughing. I felt a settling in my chest: Ellie was more than just okay. She was thriving.

"Daddy! You won't believe what happened today!" she exclaimed. She told me about her school's good morning song, the new friends she met, and the games they played. She paused only to catch her breath, describing how she had raced down the steep slide faster than anyone else.

Her stories weren't grand or heroic, but ordinary. Beautifully, gloriously ordinary. She was just being a kid, unapologetically herself, living freely in a world that had once felt so uncertain. Listening to her animated voice and laughter bubbling through each story, I realized how much she had missed this kind of normal.

Her joy reminded me of a word I've always loved - hoppipolla. It's an Icelandic term that literally means "jumping into puddles," but its meaning runs deeper. In 2005, the Icelandic band Sigur Rós released a song by that name, an ethereal hymn to childlike wonder, simplicity, and joy. The music video shows elderly men and women laughing, splashing in puddles, playing pranks, and rediscovering the delight of being alive.

Hoppipolla captures something essential: the way joy hides in ordinary moments, waiting for us to notice. It's a reminder that wonder doesn't disappear with age; we just forget where to look. Children never hesitate to leap into puddles. They won't worry about muddy shoes or soaked jeans. They leap because it's there. Because in that brief, messy moment, life feels infinite.

Hearing Ellie talk about her first day felt like watching her jump into puddles. Every slide she went down, every new friend she made, every burst of laughter was her way of leaping. There was no fear, no overthinking, no anxiety about the next moment. There was simply joy in the present. And in her joy, she invited us to leap too.

Because life isn't measured by how carefully we step around the puddles. It's measured by how fully we leap into them. The point was never to stay dry. It was to embrace the splash.

And that's exactly what Ellie had done her entire life. From the time she was in infant, her bright, talkative personality found ways to fill the room with light. Leukemia dimmed that glow for a season, but it never extinguished it. Even in the darkest of moments of the past year, she never lost her spark. Her laughter still rang out. Her curiosity still led her forward. Her light still reached us.

Now, as she stepped into this new chapter of her life, she was showing us yet again that joy doesn't wait for ideal conditions. Ellie had always been leaping: through hospital corridors, through long nights of treatment, and now across the playground on her very first day of school. She wasn't just teaching us how to embrace the splash; she was reminding us that she had been doing it all along.

As 2024 drew to a close, that spark only grew brighter. What once felt like a distant dream was now unfolding before us: Ellie's treatment was nearing its end. One by one, the pill bottles that once lined our kitchen countertops began to disappear. Each empty bottle tossed into the trash became a tiny celebration. They were no longer a symbol of what she had endured; they were a symbol of what was beginning.

There were still milestones ahead: final chemotherapy appointments, the removal of Ellie's port, and the long-awaited bell ringing ceremony. But we no longer lived in anticipation of them. Instead, we made our own milestones. We circled days on the calendar when certain medications would run out, and celebrated with cake or impromptu dance parties. Rosie made drawings and beaded bracelets for Ellie to mark each step. Together, we decided to live in the uncertainty, rather than be ruled by it.

One particularly warm winter morning, we went to a local park to kick a soccer ball around. By now, any time Ellie played soccer, she treated it like a televised event. She wore her Charlotte F.C. jersey, laced up her sneakers, and even did a full warm up before the first kick. When the ball finally rolled, she was all focus and determination. She dribbled the soccer ball with ease and grace, heading toward the goal at full speed before blasting a shot into the bottom right corner of the net. Each time she scored, she celebrated as though she'd just won the World Cup. There was jumping, cheering, and even a knee slide.

Watching her that morning, I couldn't help but think back to her honorary captaincy at the Charlotte F.C. match. So much had changed since then. Ellie no longer looked like a child battling leukemia; her face was full again, her hair had nearly all grown back, and her once pale complexion was now a distant memory. Even her medical outlook had transformed. A year ago, every lab result filled us with dread. Now, we looked forward to them.

But watching Ellie play soccer at the park that morning, I found myself more focused on what *hadn't* changed. Whether it was a stadium filled with cheering fans or an empty field with just us, Ellie carried herself the same way. At the Charlotte F.C. match, she had sprinted onto the field with the confidence of a seasoned captain. Here, at the neighborhood park with no fans and no scoreboard, she did the very same. Back then, she celebrated a goal in front of thousands; here, she celebrated just as fiercely with no one else watching. Stadium or park, professional match or quiet morning, it didn't matter. She was still Ellie. If leukemia - or her recovery from it - was supposed to change who Ellie was, no one had told her.

Leukemia never defined who Ellie was, and hadn't change who she is. Ellie is herself *in spite of* leukemia, not because of it.

People often search for silver linings in her diagnosis. They insist that the pain and suffering was somehow useful, that it will shape the woman she will one day become. They say leukemia made her resilient, brave, and empathetic. They talk as if her personality bloomed from the foot of a hospital bed. As if we should somehow be grateful for the needles, the fevers, the sleepless nights, and the side effects. As if the cancer made her who she is today.

That is as absurd as it is false.

Leukemia didn't create resilience or bravery or empathy. If anything, it handed Ellie every excuse in the world to stop showing up, to retreat, to let the world move on without her. She would have been forgiven for feeling different from other kids, for fearing each one of the hundreds of clinic visits, or for lamenting the unfairness of it all. She was just a child. Any of that would have been normal.

But she never took those excuses. She kept laughing. She kept playing. She kept leaping into life with both feet. There wasn't a single clinic visit that added bravery to her arsenal, no procedure that manufactured empathy.

Make no mistake: cancer takes away from us all. It steals time, energy, and innocence. There is no silver lining. There is no gratitude to be found in the diagnosis. We will never be thankful for the genetic blip that brought years of unimaginable pain to our innocent child.

The cancer didn't define her strength; it revealed what was already there.

And that's the truth so many miss: adversity doesn't create character, it unmasks it. The diagnosis didn't gift Ellie bravery. It stripped everything else away until all that remained *was* her bravery. That's who she has always been, long before leukemia tried to claim her.

And perhaps that's the larger truth: hardship doesn't make us who we are, it only reveals who we've always been. Ellie was resilient before leukemia. She was empathetic before the needles and the procedures. The disease didn't plant those seeds. If anything, it tried to rip them out. But if this period of our lives taught us anything, it's that even a deadly diagnosis couldn't uproot who Ellie has always been.

As we neared the end of her treatment, the little girl we had always known came fully into view again. At school, teachers couldn't stop talking about her humor, curiosity, and kindness. At home, Ellie and Rosie played endlessly, inventing games and whispering secrets at bedtime. She was fiercely competitive and stubborn too, always demanding the best of herself and eager to learn more.

By Thanksgiving, her energy was unstoppable. She darted from room to room, telling jokes, drawing turkeys, and making sure Rosie followed her lead in every game. Every corner of the house buzzed with her imagination and joy. In those moments, it was unmistakably clear: leukemia hadn't changed her. It only illuminated the boundless, fearless, and unapologetically vibrant person she had always been.

Life was beginning to feel whole again, like we were reclaiming the normalcy we had craved for so long. As the new year approached, we faced one final milestone: Ellie's port removal. It was a procedure we had long awaited, marked by equal parts relief and quiet nerves. But for the first time, the medical procedure didn't fill me with dread. It felt like the last step in a journey we had already survived. We were ready to watch her take this one last leap, to close the door on a chapter we never asked to write.

The morning of the port removal felt strangely calm. To Ellie, it was just another day. She knew the significance of the moment and had counted down to it for weeks, but she didn't dwell on it. She marched into the hospital as if it were the championship game, eager to get things started.

I hugged her tight as she made her way into the operating room, her little body swallowed by the oversized gown that made her look even smaller. I felt the weight of her bravery press against my chest in that hug, a reminder that she carried us just as much as we carried her. She didn't cry or cling. She walked with that familiar bounce in her step, waving to the nurses as if she were headed to a stage instead of a sterile operating table.

When the hallway doors swung shut, I stood frozen for a moment, caught between pride and the ache of letting her go. Even for something as necessary and celebratory as this, it still crushed me to watch her disappear down that hall.

The procedure itself was quick, almost anticlimactic compared to everything that had come before it. When they wheeled her back into the room, groggy and immediately requesting a cake pop, Emily and I finally allowed ourselves to breathe.

For once, there was no next treatment. No looming clinic schedule. No countdown to the next dose. Just quiet. Just relief.

There would be a period of recovery, of course. Ellie would need a few days of rest for the surgical wound to heal. But beyond that, there was only freedom.

For years, our lives had been structured around blood counts, appointments, and side effects. Suddenly, the calendar was empty. The hospital, which had almost become a second home, no longer dictated our days. It was liberating, yes, but also unnerving. We had spent so long in survival mode that the idea of a "normal life" felt unfamiliar, almost foreign.

And yet, in the weeks that followed, we began to feel the difference. Bedtimes became simpler. Mornings, less frantic. We made plans without double-checking with an oncologist. Ellie laughed louder, played harder, and carried herself with confidence. She still had to see doctors periodically for lab work, but it was standard procedure for someone newly out of treatment. All signs pointed toward a clear recovery. No surprises.

A few short weeks after her port removal, the day finally arrived: Ellie's 'Ring the Bell' ceremony.

The bell ringing is a shared tradition across hospitals. Patients, family, friends, and medical staff gather to celebrate the end of cancer treatment.

It had been 856 days since the day Ellie was diagnosed with leukemia. In a moment, every parent's worst nightmare became our reality. What followed were, without question, the toughest two years of our lives.

Those years were filled with very dark moments. We spent the first month living out of a hospital room. We made hundreds of hospital trips, including long overnight stays and emergency room check ins. We survived high fevers, severe side effects, and a kind of emotional exhaustion we could never have imagined.

Throughout this experience, we asked ourselves 'Why Ellie? Why our family? Why leukemia?' It was tempting to look for a cause behind the suffering, to find someone or something to blame. For others, it was equally tempting to be comforted by the idea that 'everything happens for a reason.'

But the truth is, no one is owed a reason.

Each one of us lives on the fortunate side of the universe's entropy. There are infinite tragedies that could have struck us but didn't. No one *chose* to be born where they were born. Any one of us could have entered the world in a place where a preventable disease would take our life before we ever spoke a word. A random genetic mutation could have made our story much shorter. A brain aneurysm could have ended it before this sentence.

As the Stoics remind us, living with the awareness of all that could have been reframes how we see what is. Every 'Why us?' can be followed by an equal number of 'Why nots.'

Unfortunately, randomness and chance dealt Ellie a bad hand. There is no one to blame and there is no divine plan in place. This hardship can fall upon anyone at any time, for no reason beyond chance.

But we found solace not in asking why, but asking how. How do we keep showing up, even in the face of despair? How do we carry what we've endured without letting it define us? How do we make the most of each moment, regardless of the circumstance, to enjoy a fulfilling life? How can we take the next step forward?

The *why* will never have an answer. The *how* is ours to live, day by day. And in that, we discovered the only redemption hardship ever offers: the chance to remain fully human, even when the world gives you every reason not to be.

The battle is never finished. Every regular check up, every blood test, every time Ellie looks a bit more pale than usual will bring flashes of fear and memories of what once was. We'll carry that with us for the rest of our lives. But it will no longer define us entirely.

The framework we forged through those nights in the hospital, through countless procedures and endless waiting, has become part of us. It taught us not just how to endure, but how to live.

We learned to anchor ourselves not in certainty but in presence. To laugh even when fear sat heavy in the room. To celebrate even when the outcome was unknown. That framework is what will carry us forward, long after the final medicine bottle has been thrown away and Ellie's port removed.

Ellie's story is not one of tragedy or of divine intervention, but of the relentless persistence of being human. Of splashing in puddles when the ground is soaked. Of celebrating goals no matter the size of the field. Of refusing to let the worst thing be the only thing.

But throughout this experience, we've walked down hospital hallways lined with children who won't be as lucky as Ellie. Undoubtedly, someone will write a story like this that won't end as joyfully. That truth will always stay with us. It reminds us of the fragility of these moments and the ways in which randomness didn't take everything from us.

It's why we hold each hug a little tighter, laugh a little longer, and never miss a bedtime kiss goodnight.

And so, on the morning Ellie was set to ring the bell, she asked for chocolate chip pancakes to celebrate. 856 days earlier, I would have given my life for the promise of making pancakes for a cancer-free Ellie one day. But that morning, we had exactly that: a happy, healthy five year old who wanted extra chocolate chips in her pancakes. On the day we had circled on our calendar for over two years, Ellie was getting whatever she wanted.

And in true Ellie fashion, she let the day to come and go. We celebrated with her favorite dinner and cake, let her stay up past her bedtime, and told her how proud we were. But by the time we tucked her in bed, she was already onto the next thing. She talked about school the next day, a new game she wanted to play with Rosie, and what she might have for breakfast in the morning.

For her, this wasn't the closing of a chapter. It was simply another day to live, laugh, and leap forward.

For us, though, the milestone wasn't just another day; it was proof of how far Ellie had come, and how much more there was to look forward to. That's what made the Make-A-Wish trip to Disney so perfectly timed.

It wasn't a capstone to her journey, but a launchpad. It was a chance for Ellie to step fully into childhood again, to trade hospital gowns for princess dresses, IV poles for castle parades, and clinic rooms for merry-go-rounds. It was *the* place to simply be a kid. For Emily and me, it was a reminder that our family could look forward without always looking back.

We made the most of every moment at Disney. Ellie and Rosie went on every ride they were tall enough for, their laughter echoing through roller coasters and spinning teacups. We stayed at each park from dawn until dusk, following our curiosity wherever it led. One minute we were hugging Disney characters and twirling with princesses, the next we were walking among kangaroos at Animal Kingdom. We even watched a rocket launch from the nearby Kennedy Space Center, the girls proudly announcing they wanted to be scientists one day. Every corner held a new adventure, and Ellie threw herself into each one with fearless delight.

For us, it wasn't just about castles or rides. It was about watching Ellie and Rosie reclaim what so many hospital days had stolen: unfiltered joy, boundless imagination, and the freedom to be little girls chasing their next adventure.

As our final night settled in, we gathered on Main Street with thousands of others, waiting for the fireworks to begin. We had been there since early morning, and the girls were wiped. Rosie rested her head on Emily's shoulder while Ellie wrapped her arms around my waist. It was dark now, long past their bedtime, but their eyes still flickered with anticipation.

When the first burst of color cracked the sky, Ellie's head tilted back, eyes wide, mouth open in wonder. Her arms tightened around me while Rosie lifted her head off Emily's shoulder, just in time to catch the next bloom of light.

Though the fireworks were mesmerizing, I couldn't help but steal glances at Ellie. Each boom and burst made her eyes widen, reflecting the colors that danced across the sky. Every sparkle seemed to mirror her expression, amazed at the spectacle unfolding above. As the light traced shadows through her curls, I thought about everything we had been through to reach this moment.

To Ellie and Rosie, the fireworks were just another unforgettable piece of the best week of their lives. To me, it felt like something even greater. The show was a marker of all we had endured: the fear, the hotel room, the hospital rooms, the waiting, the tears, the torment of life's unanswered questions, the lab results, the uncertainty. But it was also a reminder of what we experienced in spite of the chaos: the kindness of strangers, the generosity of loved ones, the steadfast support of so many, the wonders of modern science, the sound of the bell ringing.

And now, here we were, standing in a sea of hope. The world around us was erupting not in chaos, but in celebration. Each burst was brief, brilliant, unforgettable, and then gone in an instant. That's the truth about fireworks: their beauty exists because they don't last. Maybe that's the truth of life, too. We don't get to hold on to these moments forever, but while they're here, they can light up everything around us.

And that, I had come to realize, was okay with me. That night, standing there with Ellie's armed wrapped tight around me, I didn't need forever. I just needed that moment.

The finale came and went, and the night sky fell quiet again. We made our way toward the park's exit, Ellie and Rosie still smiling through their tired yawns. In the stillness that followed, it struck me that life's meaning isn't found in the fireworks of all, but in what remains after the echoes fade.

However incredible the show was, it couldn't match the beauty of the quiet moments that followed. Over the past two years, we made it through the bursts and booms, the darkness and the light, and the full spectrum of human emotion. Cancer hadn't given us meaning, nor had it left us with answers. It stripped life to its core, revealing what was always there but too often overlooked: the strength hidden in the small moments like this one and the unshakable love that binds us together.

We walked on beneath the dim glow of streetlights, hands clasped tightly together. Tomorrow would bring its own memories, its own battles, its own unknowns. But for tonight, we carried the quiet certainty that through it all, we can endure.

Epilogue

No one really prepares you for the pageantry of a preschool graduation. One minute you're dropping your kid off with a lunchbox packed neatly with a peanut butter and jelly sandwich, and the next you're sitting in a gymnasium-turned-auditorium, watching a sea of five year olds parade in wearing oversized gowns. Ellie spotted us right away, and the whole crowd spotted her too. It was hard not to. The graduation cap that looked oversized for every other kid seemed to float on Ellie's full mane of curls.

Emily and I picked a row of folding chairs and sat Rosie beside us as the lights dimmed and a projector flickered to life. A slideshow of first-day-of-school photos filled the screen. Some kids ran toward the building, low-hanging backpacks bouncing behind them, eager to get started. Others lingered by the door, flashing anxious smiles at the camera. Then Ellie's photo appeared, taken just nine months early; for a moment, I hardly recognized her.

Her curls had only just started to grow back, hanging loosely over her ears. She looked thinner, paler. Even in those final months of her treatment, she still carried the signs of chemotherapy side effects.

But as the slideshow continued, Ellie began to reemerge. With each new photo, her hair thickened, her face filled out, and her shoulders straightened. Most of all, her smile grew wider. The nervous grin from her first day gave way to a full-on belly laugh on the playground. We were watching her recovery unfold right there on the screen.

Just a few weeks earlier, I'd been in this same gym with Ellie for our first father-daughter dance. She wore a fluffy pink dress and sparkly clips that she said made her look "fancy." From the minute we walked in, she spun, jumped, and laughed across the dance floor.

We had made it through two songs before she ran off to play with friends. I watched her dash across the gym, pink dress puffing out like a parachute, hair clips barely hanging on. In true Ellie fashion, the night was less about slow dances and more about squeezing every ounce of fun out of the evening.

But when the DJ announced the final song, she came sprinting back toward me. She stood on my shoes, wrapped her arms around my legs, and squeezed tight.

"Best. Night. Ever," she declared.

I'm not sure how much credit I deserved, given how little of the night she spent with me, but I didn't argue. Just having that moment, our first father-daughter dance together, was enough to agree with her claim.

And now, here she was, leaving this school behind. Next year would bring kindergarten, and Ellie wouldn't be a preschooler anymore. Every parent knows it's impossible to stop seeing your child as the baby they once were, and I was starting to feel it too. With each passing day, the gap between who she was and who she was becoming seemed to widen. The little girl who once clung to my leg now marched into classrooms with confidence, made friends on her own, and told stories with a wit that felt far beyond her years. It was thrilling to watch, and bittersweet too. She was moving forward, whether I was ready or not.

But I was ready. As much as I missed the snuggle stage of infancy or the wobbling walk of toddlerhood, I've always preferred each new age to the one before it. As Ellie and Rosie grow, I love learning who they are. I love our conversations, their humor, their curiosity, and the way they think. Every day is an invitation to discover who they're becoming, and I couldn't be prouder.

So when Ellie walked across the preschool graduation stage, I had to take a deep breath to keep from crying. I wondered if every milestone would feel like this. The lump in your throat, the sting in your eyes, the ache of knowing it's all moving too fast. But beneath all of that was something stronger: gratitude.

There was a time, back in that hotel room in Charlotte, when none of this felt certain. I didn't know if I'd ever sit in a folding chair watching my daughter in a bright red graduation cap. I didn't know if there would ever be a father-daughter dance. I didn't know if I'd ever see her wave proudly from the stage.

But here I was. Somehow, we endured.

When I first told friends and family I was writing a book about Ellie's treatment, I said my only hope was that it might help someone else facing something traumatic. What I didn't realize until I finished it was that, more than anything, it helped me. Writing became a way to make sense of what had happened, to put words around the chaos and give shape to the pain. It reminded me of how far we've come, and how much strength was forged in the middle of fear. If this book helps others, I'll be grateful. But even if it never leaves these pages, I'll still be thankful for what it gave me.

What carried us through wasn't luck or blind optimism, though it's undeniable that randomness ultimately tilted in our favor in the end. More importantly, we endured by focusing on what we could control, refusing to let fear define us, and anchoring ourselves in a framework that carried us through the toughest of days.

The many words I've written about this framework pale beside those penned millennia ago by Marcus Aurelius:

"Never let the future disturb you. You will meet it, if you have to, with the same weapons of reason which today arm you in the present."

The Stoic philosopher reminds us that the tools we use to navigate the present are the same ones that will guide us through the future. That single line captures the essence of what carried us through Ellie's treatment: to approach each moment deliberately, armed with reason and presence. It's not just a philosophy for surviving hardship - it's a framework for living fully, even when life feels unpredictable. Because in the end, reason is all we have. It's humanity's sharpest tool, ready for whatever challenge lies ahead.

With that in mind, I've distilled this approach into a simple, step-by-step blueprint that anyone can use to face uncertainty, regain control, and cultivate resilience in their own life. It doesn't require a cancer diagnosis or a crisis. I use it every day, from major life decisions to the smallest of moments.

Step 1: Recognize what is happening.
Strip away the narrative and the noise. What's true right now? What do I know for sure? Ground yourself in facts before feelings.

Step 2: Choose your lens.
The story you tell shapes the life you live. Define what's happening based purely on the facts from Step 1. Craft that narrative clearly and deliberately; nothing influences your mental state more than the story you choose to believe.

Step 3: This happened, now what?
Focus on the smallest manageable window. What needs to happen in the next five minutes? Separate the controllable from the uncontrollable. Act only on what's within your reach. Ask yourself: what's the next thing I can do that moves me toward my goal?

Step 4: Act with purpose and precision.
Be deliberate. Apply reason, logic, and discipline. Move forward, no matter how small the step. Execution is the bridge between resilience and results.

Step 5: Anchor in purpose.
When clarity wavers, return to what motivates you: your values, your loved ones, your sense of meaning. Purpose is the fuel for persistence.

Step 6: Reflect and refine.
Create a space to reflect after the storm. What did you learn? How did you grow? What will you do differently next time? Reflection turns experience into evolution.

What you've read in these pages was my attempt to apply this framework to Ellie's journey. I still have a lot to learn, but I'm improving each day. The framework isn't a destination, it's a practice. The challenges, uncertainties, and moments ahead will bring new opportunities to grow. The work is ongoing, and that's both humbling and invigorating.

The truth is, there will be days ahead that are immensely rewarding and others that will test us in ways we couldn't have imagined. But armed with the blueprint I've shared, I feel ready to face whatever life throws our way.

And while this book captures the lessons we've learned and the framework that's guided us, it also reminded me that strength isn't meant to be contained. The resilience, courage, and joy we witnessed in Ellie inspired action, and it was Emily who brought that inspiration to life. I am endlessly proud of her for creating the Strong Like Ellie Foundation, turning our daughter's journey into a source of hope and support for other families facing the unimaginable.

Emily continues to inspire me every day. Late at night, after the kids are asleep and the house grows quiet, she flips on the light in her office and gets to work helping others. She founded the organization on a simple but profound belief: no family should have to walk the childhood cancer journey alone. The foundation provides everyday, practical support for local families caught in the storm of diagnosis - from hand-made tote bags filled with clinic visit essentials to grocery store gift cards and customized port-friendly tee shirts. It's about bringing a little light to the everyday moments that can feel impossibly heavy.

Most importantly, the Strong Like Ellie Foundation creates connection. Families navigating childhood cancer often feel isolated, adrift in a world that can't quite understand their reality. Like this book, the foundation turns Ellie's story into a lifeline, a simple way of saying *"you are not alone."*

That's what makes it so meaningful. It's not just about honoring what Ellie went through; it's about acknowledging what families continue to go through, even after the last hospital bracelet comes off. The randomness of it all never really leaves you.

Because Ellie's story, like so many others, didn't end when treatment did. Life after cancer, for those lucky enough to have one, isn't a clean break. There's no neat line separating the *before* and *after*. She still goes to doctor's visits. We still find ourselves holding our breath when she coughs or looks pale. The fear never fully leaves, it just doesn't overtake us anymore. The framework helps navigate the uncertainty, but it's our connection with others that truly puts everything into perspective.

The Stoics are often misunderstood as being detached from emotion, as if wisdom requires coldness. But that's not the truth. Ancient Stoics distinguished between two kinds of emotion: *Apatheia,* freedom from irrational passions that are disruptive or excessive, and *Eupatheiai,* rational, healthy emotions like joy, caution, or compassion.

Apatheia doesn't mean becoming a stone. It doesn't mean you stop feeling or detach from the people you love. It means you strip away the irrational passions that cloud judgment and make suffering heavier than it already is. The goal is to move away from the fear that paralyzes you, the anger that lashes out, and the despair that insists tomorrow can't be endured.

What remains, the eupatheiai, are the healthier emotions. The joy of doing what's right, the caution that keeps you alert but not panicked, and the love expressed through reason and presence rather than possession and fear.

That distinction became real for me during Ellie's leukemia journey. I couldn't afford to collapse under anxiety or let grief take the wheel. But I also couldn't shut down. I had to feel. I had to love, protect, and encourage her. And I found that I could do that most effectively when my emotions were grounded in reason, not the other way around. The clearest, most peaceful moments came when I made a conscious choice to hold onto joy, patience, and gratitude instead of fear or resentment. They came in the quiet decision to show up each day, in a hospital room or at home, and be steady, armed with reason.

But we didn't do it alone. Whatever strength we managed to find was never just ours. We were held up by an extraordinary network of family and fiends. They showed up in a hundred unseen ways, carrying us through the darkest of hours. I'll never forget the surprise cross-country visits from Emily's brothers and sister. I'll always remember getting pictures and videos of Rosie saying goodnight, send by our parents and in-laws while we sat with Ellie in an emergency room. They became our safety net, stepping in when we were too tired to think straight, reminding us that we didn't have to carry everything by ourselves.

I have an immense appreciation for the doctors, nurses, and researchers who gave us more than just Ellie's treatment. They gave us hope. Hope rooted in science, in progress, and in the relentless human drive to push medicine forward. On the day of the diagnosis, a doctor told us that fifty years earlier, this would have been a death sentence. It's because of the scientific and medical community that Ellie will start kindergarten this fall, with her whole life ahead of her.

And somehow, that community gave us more than just survival. They made Ellie smile in her darkest moments. They steadied us when fear threatened to take over. We were reminded of this through every laugh from a nurse who knew Ellie's quirks, every late-night reassurance that she would be okay, and every tip that helped us get through the next round of chemotherapy side effects.

These voices of reason never offered divine guarantees or planned explanations. They offered something truer, a grounded kind of hope. The belief that we could face whatever was ahead, no matter what tomorrow held. There were days we couldn't see it yet, and nights when we weren't sure we could endure another setback. But their presence, their calm, and their knowledge is what carried us through.

In the end, this story is not just about cancer. It isn't a how-to guide for navigating leukemia. It's a story about learning to see clearly, to choose our lens, and to keep moving forward even when the road crumbles beneath our feet. It's about the power of family, of community, and of modern science all converging to give a little girl her life back. But most of all, it's a story about how we endured.

I can't pretend to know what tomorrow holds. None of us can. But today, Ellie laughs with Rosie, makes plans for the weekend, and dreams like any child should. Today, Emily and I hold each other a little closer, grateful for science, for family, and for life itself, even with all its randomness. And today, that's enough.

If this book leaves you with anything, I hope it is this: strength is not the absence of fear, but the decision to keep showing up. It's the conscious effort to show up again and again for the people we love, for the values we hold, and for the moments that matter most.

The fight changed us, but it did not break us. We are here. We are present. And we are Strong Like Ellie.

About the Author

Louie Bottone is a father, husband, and writer whose work bridges lived experience and the quiet guidance of philosophy His debut book, What We Can Endure grew from the hardest season of his life — his daughter's fight with leukemia — and the search for a way to stay steady, present, and human through it all.

Drawing on a background in learning and leadership development, Louie explores how ideas become practices, and how reflection can become resilience. His writing invites readers to see philosophy not as a distant discipline, but as a companion in suffering, a guide for endurance, and a path toward presence.

He lives in North Carolina with his wife and two daughters, where he continues to write about meaning, endurance, and the daily work of becoming whole.

FOUNDATION

At Strong Like Ellie Foundation, we believe that no family should walk the childhood cancer journey alone. Our mission is to provide hope, comfort, and tangible support to families navigating the unimaginable challenges of pediatric cancer.

Whether you are a parent, caregiver, supporter, or simply someone who cares, you are welcome here. This space was created to offer resources, encouragement, and connection. We know that together, we are stronger.

We invite you to explore our upcoming fundraisers, learn how you can make a difference, and join a compassionate community dedicated to lifting up strong children and the families who love them.

Thank you for being a part of this mission. Your presence here matters. Who is your reason to be strong?

Learn more at www.stronglikeellie.org